Advance Praise for *Career Confusion*

"A recurring theme in Wilen's books is that—regardless of rank or salary level—employees need to actively shape their own career success. Put that wisdom to work by reading *Career Confusion* and come away knowing what steps you can start taking today to make your career more rewarding for a lifetime."

Caroline Molina-Ray, Ph.D., co-editor of *Women Lead:*
Career Perspectives from Workplace Leaders

"Dr. Tracey Wilen presents a vivid and compelling narrative of our journey into the 'Fourth Industrial Revolution'—the current, ever-changing digital world that is rapidly and fundamentally transforming how business, educational institutions and workers succeed. *Career Confusion* provides a clear delineation of the current major cultural, quality of life and career paradigm shifts and provides tactical and practical suggestions and resources for finding and extending successful and rewarding careers. This book is significant reading for anyone in business, human capital management, education, or career counselling."

Patricia Deasy, Practice Director, SpearMC Consulting

"This book is required reading for anyone in career transition. Navigating the inevitable career confusion that we will all experience at some point in our lives can be overwhelming and, well, confusing. Dr. Wilen walks us through this ever-changing landscape and guides us through every step of the process of pursuing a job in this modern world. The book is an invaluable resource for those just starting out, and for experienced professionals looking to make a change."

Anne Angelopoulous, Senior Director, JustStaff Inc.

"Whether you're navigating your career or managing an organization, *Career Confusion* is the best book I have read that explains the challenges and skills needed to be successful through the four Industrial Revolutions—and most importantly, the current terrain. It provides you the insights to best prepare for future employment and appreciate the roles of recruiters, career centers, corporations, and educational institutions. And it will motivate you to be a life-long learner."

Glen Fowler, 2017–18 President, National Association of Colleges and Employers

"Dr. Wilen presents a no-nonsense, factual manner to discuss how people today can manage their careers in a disrupted world. As the world continues to rapidly change, and become increasingly competitive and technical, workers will need to constantly re-evaluate their skills. Moreover, they will need to be relevant with the modern-day workforce. She offers excellent advice and recommendations for workers in all stages of their career."

Gary Daugenti, President, Gent & Associates, Inc.

"There is nothing more soul-crushing to my field than unrealized human potential. Imagine what our world could be, how much more we could accomplish and how much more satisfying our experiences would be if we all moved just a few steps closer toward identifying and achieving our individual potential. Now imagine combining that individual power with the unique potential of others, or even better: augmenting our insight on how we identify, develop and combine our skills using technologies like artificial intelligence (AI). That is an example of scalable learning and I believe that is our greatest competitive advantage."

Christine Menard, a vice president of learning and development
and a global asset manager

"If you want to stay ahead of the job curve, read this book. Dr. Tracey Wilen provides a view over the horizon. You'll find timely intel for professionals seeking insights on what trends will create job opportunities. If you are considering a new profession or looking to advance, here's the information you need to know."

John Scally, APR, MA, MPA, Media Relations Manager, Padilla

"I have admired Tracey's mastery of the business world for many years. She is keen on how companies and careers change faster than ever, the impact on lives, and the opportunity it presents. If you are student or professional and need some next step guidance—and ignore this opportunity you will be left behind. Take advantage of Tracey's vast experience and caring knowledge of the why this change happens, what it means to you, and how to thrive in today's business world. Like almost no one else Tracey can impart her wisdom in a practical and action-taking manner. She is caring, authentic, and has some brilliant advice for you. She has lived this change. Do not waste this chance—enjoy this book and keep up with time."

Derek Hibbard, Chief Marketing Officer, Fiction Tribe

Career Confusion

This book is part of the Peter Lang Education list.
Every volume is peer reviewed and meets
the highest quality standards for content and production.

PETER LANG
New York • Bern • Berlin
Brussels • Vienna • Oxford • Warsaw

Dr. Tracey Wilen

Career Confusion

21st Century Career Management in a Disrupted World

PETER LANG
New York • Bern • Berlin
Brussels • Vienna • Oxford • Warsaw

Library of Congress Cataloging-in-Publication Data

Name: Wilen, Tracey, author.
Title: Career confusion: 21st century career management
in a disrupted world / Dr. Tracey Wilen.
Description: New York: Peter Lang, 2018.
Includes bibliographical references.
Identifiers: LCCN 2018028672 | ISBN 978-1-4331-5846-9 (hardback: alk. paper)
ISBN 978-1-4331-5847-6 (paperback: alk. paper) | ISBN 978-1-4331-5848-3 (ebook pdf)
ISBN 978-1-4331-5849-0 (epub) | ISBN 978-1-4331-5850-6 (mobi)
Subjects: LCSH: Career development—United States—History.
Organizational change—United States—History.
Women—Employment—United States—History.
Management—Technological innovations.
Classification: LCC HF5382.5.U5 W55 2018 | DDC 650.14—dc23
LC record available at https://lccn.loc.gov/2018028672
DOI 10.3726/b14305

Bibliographic information published by **Die Deutsche Nationalbibliothek.**
Die Deutsche Nationalbibliothek lists this publication in the "Deutsche
Nationalbibliografie"; detailed bibliographic data are available
on the Internet at http://dnb.d-nb.de/.

The paper in this book meets the guidelines for permanence and durability
of the Committee on Production Guidelines for Book Longevity
of the Council of Library Resources.

TABLE OF CONTENTS

FIGURES

FOREWORD

Tracey Wilen's *Career Confusion: 21st Century Career Management in a Disrupted World* will inspire and energize readers. It is written from a historical perspective regarding disruption and evolution beginning with the First Industrial Revolution to the present. Tracey provides examples and commentary with glimpses of the future of artificial intelligence and robotics. This book is well-written and captures readers attention; I found it difficult to stop reading. It engages you as no other book on careers can do. Tracey's personal touch and injection of her own experiences is very meaningful and relevant. The reader becomes engaged not only in the historical context, but thoughtfully involved in the expansion of one's vision of the rapidly evolving career paths that will be available to those who become life-long learners. The unusual approach to the career dilemma leads the reader into the fact gathering phase of understanding organizational changes and how careers are influenced by megatrends that globally transform the corporate structure. She also focuses on workplace composition that is made up of different generational levels. This tends to present additional challenges to organizations as cultural differences and work habits are often in conflict. Against this background the author focuses the reader on the need for talent management as organizations change and career paths are altered. It is apparent that the job market is rapidly changing as the world becomes more digital. As Tracey points out, the career path you may choose today may not be available in the future. You must always be a learner and adjust to change. *Career Confusion* is a must-read for students and individuals navigating career paths. This book is one of the most enjoyable resources on the topic of career management that I have had the pleasure to read.

John P. McGowan, Ph.D.,
Vice Provost and CIO,
The University of Alabama;
Associate Vice Chancellor for IT,
The University of Alabama System

INTRODUCTION

The world has changed.

Sue worked for a large corporation that was an industry leader for many years. She felt secure in her job. During her tenure at the firm, small and agile firms opened, new competitors emerged and dominated the industry seemingly overnight. Sue's management was out of touch with the trends and resisted change. One rainy Monday in her eleventh year at the firm, Sue showed up to work to find the front doors chained closed.

Joe was a senior manager at a large firm. Joe's responsibility was to train and manage new hires. Joe was too busy with management, training, and administration that he neglected to keep up with technology, the competition, and the market trends, letting his staff do the work. His young team were quick learners, became fast climbers, and were promoted over Joe in a matter of months.

Carol, an individual marketing contributor, celebrated her fiftieth birthday on a three-week well-deserved vacation. While gone, her management hired a younger, technical, inexpensive associate to cover for her. When she returned, there were new processes in place, new initiatives, and she was eventually forced into early retirement.

Ed climbed the corporate ladder by keeping his nose to the grindstone. While he was working hard, his firm hired a young consulting team who brought in new ideas about work, automation, and technical fluency. Seemingly overnight Ed became irrelevant and considered a legacy.

Jane was a successful customer service representative. She had top ratings for her work as a customer service representative. Unbeknownst to her, one of the clients acquired the firm and her role immediately became redundant.

Allen was in the fifteenth year as the CEO of a large organization. He was externally vibrant and a focused CEO. Internally he was out of touch with his employees whose lives became increasingly complicated. Many employees had partners who worked, shared parenting responsibilities, took care of aging parents, or were raising children as a single parent. The employees demanded that Allen change his HR policies or they would leave and join a competitor who was more accommodating to employee work–life balance needs.

Jennifer was a top student with a 4.0 GPA. From the time she entered as a freshman to her senior year the employment landscape changed. Close to graduation she learned her degree was no longer relevant because hiring firms required new skills, experience, and competencies. She graduated summa cum laude but she was unemployed and had student debt.

Jeff was a tenured professor. He excelled at teaching his research. Jeff did not accept that his research was increasingly irrelevant to the workforce. As firms adopted new technologies, they required new skills, putting pressure on Jeff to update his curriculum to topics he did not understand.

Angie owned a retail business. Since she opened her store customers' expectations changed. They wanted her to be online, use social media, website ecommerce, and offer low prices like the competition. Over time, Angie found herself in debt trying to fund marketing and web advancements and meet competitive pricing demands.

Mike is in Human Resources. His job is to interview and screen candidates to match skills and experience to job requirements. He is finding that interviewees are changing and asking more about the firm's philanthropy efforts, community outreach, and their personal purpose rather than the job.

Anne is in HR; her job is to interview top students from premier schools for placement at the firm. She is finding that the students cannot communicate in full sentences, hold eye contact, or have a conversation without texting.

Jack's parents told him to aggressively pursue sports in grammar and high school so that he could be eligible for a college sports scholarship. Jill's parents told her to pursue math and science, volunteer for community projects, and pursue company internships. Today, Jack is a high school soccer coach. He was injured in his junior year of high school and could not continue playing sports. Jill is an executive at a top high-profile technology firm.

Chris's college career counselor told her, in her freshman year, to pursue Psychology because it was a versatile major and she was good with people. A new career counselor joined the school in her junior year. This counselor told her to switch her major to business because Psychology was no longer useful without an advanced degree but a business degree would get her a job. Chris changed her major and graduated in five years instead of four. She was employed one week after graduation by a notable health care firm in a business role.

Sid and Nancy worked in finance for high-tech firms. They were laid off at the same time. Both were tired of their jobs and fed up with the industry churn. Sid pursued the same finance job he had in the same industry (technology) to get back to work quickly. Nancy decided it was the perfect time to try and pursue something new, marketing, and a new industry: nonprofit. Sid secured a job in less than four weeks. His expertise and experience matched the job opening and he was the most qualified candidate for the finance jobs posted by technology firms. Nancy, after six months, is still looking for a job. Her finance expertise and technology experience do not match the marketing job requirements and new industry (nonprofit). She is competing with candidates who are more qualified for the jobs.

The world of work has changed in a very short time and this has created career confusion.

Here are some facts:

- The World Economic Forum notes 65 percent children entering primary school today will ultimately end up working in completely new job types that don't yet exist.[1]

- According to the Bureau of Labor Statistics (BLS), baby boomers held an average of 11.7 jobs by age forty-eight, with some as many as fifteen jobs.[2]
- The U.S. BLS reported 5.8 million jobs were unfilled on the last day of 2017.[3]
- Georgetown University's Center on Education and the Workforce projects there will be 55 million job openings by 2020.[4]
- According to American Enterprise Institute only 12.2 percent of Fortune 500 firms in 1955 were still in existence in 2014. Eighty-eight percent have gone bankrupt, merged, or have fallen off the list.[5]
- According to Innosight, by 2027 the average life of firms on the S&P 500 will be under 12 years.[6]
- Business Insider reports America's top ten highest-paying jobs for 2018 require STEM training and advanced degrees.[7]
- A Pew Research Center survey found that 50 percent of educators felt they needed to better prepare graduates for a highly competitive job market.[8]
- Pew Research Center reports 35 percent of educators surveyed stated they need to rethink curricula, to shift from personal growth and intellectualism to job preparation.[9]
- The World Economic Forum states the most in-demand occupations and specialties did not exist ten or even five years ago, and the pace of change will accelerate.[10]
- The BLS notes top 2018 job openings are in health care, information technology, digital services, construction, and long-haul drivers. These areas will create 5.3 million new jobs by 2022, a third of the total employment growth.[11]
- The Society for Human Resources Management reports 68 percent of U.S. HR professionals can't find qualified talent. Eighty-four percent found it even harder to locate candidates with soft skills.[12]
- Pew Research Center states employment is increasing faster for jobs that require more competencies and preparation. Workers have to be articulate in social, communication, analytical, and critical thinking skills.[13]
- *Fast Company* reports five US job categories *hardest* to fill in 2025 are: skilled trades, health care, manufacturing, sales, and math-related professions.[14]
- Pew Research Group reports that over 54 percent of employers and employees know they must focus on continuous learning with training and job reskilling, to keep up with new technological advancements.[15]

Confused? The modern day workforce problems of today's society are not unique. *Career Confusion* discusses the sequence of events, technology shifts, and transitions that have led up to today's job landscape. By reviewing prior societal revolutions in the United States the reader will gain insights on how humanity has managed through past transitions with success. The book discusses today's Fourth Industrial revolution that has created skill gaps, new training requirements, and preparation for modern careers. The book provides advice for educators and students on career planning, occupation choices, and employment strategies. *Career Confusion* provides insights to industry leaders on career development for a multigeneration workforce, education partnerships, and reskilling programs. The final chapter provides advice on how to future-proof your career at every stage of employment.

Section I: Transitions and Continuous Change

Chapter 1: The First Industrial Revolution in the United States

The world of work has changed for our generation in a very short time, in creating career confusion for young and old alike. This chapter reviews how change and career confusion is not new for society and dates back to the first Industrial revolution when the United States shifted from agriculture to factories and automation.

Chapter 2: The Second Industrial Revolution

The Second Industrial Revolution made America the world's leading industrial power. This period fueled mass advancements in agriculture, manufacturing, and transportation. New ideas and inventions such as the telephone, skyscrapers, steel, oil, railroads, automobiles, and washing machines spread rapidly, changing society, industry, and firms forever. Skill gaps, labor disputes, and massive industry growth reflect this era.

Chapter 3: The Third Industrial Revolution

The Third Industrial Revolution dramatically changed the world with the accelerated creation of digital technologies, in switching from mechanical and analog electrical technologies. Xerox, Microsoft, IBM, Apple, HP, Facebook, and Google are some of the well-known firms that emerged during this timeframe, changing the society forever. This era is often remembered marked by the dot. com period of hypergrowth and employment and the dot.bomb when firms were faced with tremendous layoffs to be repeated again in 2007 with the great recession. The Third Industrial Revolution was a key milestone; it put technology into our hands, helping us become more productive, connected, and creating different lives to reflect our own unique career goals and aspirations.

Chapter 4: The Fourth Industrial Revolution

The Fourth Industrial Revolution is the fourth major shift in the United States. It is characterized by the intersection of technologies that blur the lines between the physical, digital, and biological spheres. It is marked by emerging technology breakthroughs in robotics, artificial intelligence, nanotechnology, The Internet of Things, 3D printing, and autonomous vehicles. These new technologies will replace, displace, and create new jobs for modern society.

Section II: Forces Impacting Your Career and Employability

Chapter 5: How Key Megatrends of Change Impact Organizations and Careers

This chapter will discuss some of the key forces that are impacting organization leaders, employees, and career planning today. Increased longevity impacts individuals who will need to work longer to afford to retire, it also impacts organization leaders who have to manage five generations in the workforce. Globalization creates a much more competitive environment for organizations to survive and puts pressure on organizations to hire, develop, and retain more competitive globally savvy leaders and employees. The changing family structure increased the need for flexible work options rather than the face-to-face 9–5 workday. Diversity is the new corporate mindset.

Chapter 6: Talent Shortage and the Skills Gap

This chapter discusses the current debate on the skills gap and talent shortage felt by US employers, what skills are in demand, how to close the skill gap, and how industry and education can provide solutions.

Chapter 7: Higher Education Prepares Students for Jobs, Careers, and Life

This chapter discusses Higher Education preparing students for jobs and the role of continuous education, the emergence of online training platforms, and the increasing importance of career centers on college campuses to facilitate student employment. The chapter also discusses the impact and success of education and corporate partnerships on student opportunities and employment.

Section III: Career Planning—Preparing for Future Jobs and Careers

Chapter 8: Shifting Organizations and Talent Management

This chapter will cover shifting organization structures and impact on career path, how to develop career success for each generation, and what firms are doing to help retain employees to build their careers at the organization.

Chapter 9: Where Are the Jobs?

The World Economic Forum notes that 65 percent of children entering primary school today will ultimately end up working in a job that does not yet exist. The BLS notes there will be 55 million job openings in the economy through 2020 of which 24 million openings are from newly created jobs. The US Department of Labor *Occupational Outlook Handbook* adds hundreds of new jobs and categories every two years.

Chapter 10: Career Planning for Individuals

We are living longer and working longer. Many of us will be working for sixty or more years. This new career landscape requires planning and foresight for our journeys from identifying our interests when we are young, exploring options in high school, and taking action in college to pursuing the first job. The new landscape of finding and applying for jobs has changed due to technology. This chapter will also discuss how to future-proof your career before, during, and after the organization.

Notes

1. World Economic Forum, "The Future of Jobs and Skills," 2016, http://reports.weforum.org/future-of-jobs-2016/chapter-1-the-future-of-jobs-and-skills/.
2. Bureau of Labor Statistics, "National Longitudinal Surveys," n.d., https://www.bls.gov/nls/nlsfaqs.htm#anch41.
3. Bureau of Labor Statistics, "Job Openings and Labor Turnover Summary," March 16, 2018, https://www.bls.gov/news.release/jolts.nr0.htm.
4. Georgetown University Center on Education for the Workforce, https://cew.georgetown.edu/wp-content/uploads/2014/11/Recovery2020.Press-Release.pdf.
5. Mark J, Perry, "Fortune 500 Firms 1955 vs. 2016: Only 12% Remain," AEI, December 13, 2016, http://www.aei.org/publication/fortune-500-firms-1955-v-2016-only-12-remain-thanks-to-the-creative-destruction-that-fuels-economic-prosperity/.
6. Innosight, "2018 Corporate Longevity Forecast: Creative Destruction is Accelerating," https://www.innosight.com/insight/creative-destruction/.
7. Rachel Gillett, "The 25 Best High-paying Jobs in America for 2018," Business Insider, January 10, 2018, http://www.businessinsider.com/best-highest-paying-jobs-in-america-for-2018-2018-1.
8. Pew Research Center, https://assets.pewresearch.org/wp-content/uploads/sites/3/2016/10/ST_2016.10.06_Future-of-Work_FINAL4.pdf.
9. Ibid.
10. World Economic Forum, http://www3.weforum.org/docs/WEF_FOJ_Executive_Summary_Jobs.pdf.
11. Bureau of Labor Statistics, "Occupational Employment Projections to 2022," December 2013, https://www.bls.gov/opub/mlr/2013/article/occupational-employment-projections-to-2022.htm.
12. SHRM, https://www.shrm.org/hr-today/trends-and-forecasting/research-and-surveys/Documents/SHRM%20New%20Talent%20Landscape%20Recruiting%20Difficulty%20Skills.pdf.
13. Pew Research Center, https://assets.pewresearch.org/wp-content/uploads/sites/3/2016/10/ST_2016.10.06_Future-of-Work_FINAL4.pdf.
14. Gwen Moran, "5 Jobs That Will Be the Hardest to Fill in 2025," *Fast Company*, July 18, 2016, https://www.fastcompany.com/3061872/5-jobs-that-will-be-the-hardest-to-fill-in-2025.
15. Pew Research Group, https://assets.pewresearch.org/wp-content/uploads/sites/3/2016/10/ST_2016.10.06_Future-of-Work_FINAL4.pdf.

SECTION I
TRANSITIONS AND CONTINUOUS CHANGE

· 1 ·

THE FIRST INDUSTRIAL REVOLUTION
IN THE UNITED STATES

The world of work has changed for the 21st-century generation in a very short time, in creating career confusion for young and old alike. We remember our dads and granddads working for the same companies for years, then retiring with good pensions. We remember our moms and grandmothers working as teachers, nurses, and secretaries in the same jobs until they retired, often with pensions and health benefits.

When we started college we often studied courses similar to what our parents studied: business, banking, insurance, medicine, dentistry, teaching, nursing, psychology, social work, and secretarial. But upon graduating we found the world had changed and skills learned in college were often not relevant, with careers we'd chosen not what we expected them to be. What happened? We may think we're the only generation to face a rapidly changing world but generations before us also had their worlds change rapidly and were forced to rethink their lives.

Impact on Farmers

Early civilization was mainly agricultural. Imagine yourself a farmer during the First Industrial Revolution in the United States (1790–1870). You grew your own food, plowed your small field by hand, raised some livestock, and depended on your spouse and children to work the farm with you. You canned produce for winter and salted meat to preserve it. You had a loom and spun cotton into thread to make clothes for your family. In the winter, you built furniture, utensils, wagons, and other products needed on the farm or that could be traded or sold to neighbors.

You relied on your neighbors for emergencies and generally helped each other out. You weren't rich but you could feed, clothe, and provide shelter for your family. In general, you lived in a rural community and were self-sustaining.

If you lived in the South, you grew cotton and tobacco and put your family to work in the fields growing, tending, and harvesting these crops. If you had some surplus cash, you could buy a slave or two to help with the work. But then things began to change as the First Industrial Revolution in the United States saw a transition to new manufacturing processes.

Although Britain's Industrial Revolution began during the middle of the 18th century, America didn't keep pace with England in part "because the abundance of land and scarcity of labor in the New World reduced interest in expensive investments in machine production."[1] Samuel Slater, often called the "Father of the American Industrial Revolution," brought new manufacturing technologies from Britain to America and opened the first U.S. cotton mill in Pawtucket, Rhode Island, in 1790. Unlike other people who had come to the United States from England with textile manufacturing experience, Slater knew how to build and operate the machines he needed in his mill. With this new technology, Slater was able to speed up the process of spinning cotton thread into yarn.[2]

In 1794, Eli Whitney invented the cotton gin, a simple manually cranked device that mechanically removed sticky green seeds from short staple cotton. Suddenly, if you were a planter in the South, you could grow and sell much more cotton, which allowed you to buy more slaves to help in the fields.[3] Water-powered textile factories in the Northeast quickly turned raw cotton into cloth, and technology increased the demand for cotton. That meant if you were a white Southerner you began moving farther west past the Mississippi River to grow cotton to meet this increasing demand.[4]

Across America, you began to see the shift from home and hand production to machine and factory production of goods. Replacing skilled workers with machines allowed goods to multiply cheaper and faster. This shift changed a mainly agricultural society into one controlled by manufacturing and industry. This shift from products that were manmade to those made by machines ushered in a new era where the increase in productivity produced a much higher standard of living than your ancestors had been accustomed to in the preindustrial world.[5]

As a farmer who lived farther away from these new cities, you had to produce crops and other food that could be transported long distances to market. So, you started grinding wheat into flour, raising cattle you could walk to market, or pigs you could slaughter for pork. If you didn't change the way you operated your farm, you'd go out of business because you wouldn't have enough customers.[6]

In addition, new scientific methods of cultivation as well as increasing use of machines produced record crop yields, causing prices to plummet. As your costs to grow crops increased, you lost money and found yourself deep in debt. Soon, you could no longer maintain your farm, which had most likely been in your family for years.

And you realized that if you moved to the Midwest or to the thriving industrial cities of the East, you could participate in the rising prosperity. In these urban centers, you could find higher paying jobs and likely live a better life.[7] As a farmer who thought your life was all planned out, you were suddenly faced with career confusion. Where did you go from there? Which of your farming skills were transferable to the new economy? As more people were hired to work in the mills, they looked to the rural farms for milk and dairy products, vegetables, fruits, and hay for their horses. If you lived in the central New York area you began growing more specialized products, such as potatoes, barley, and hops, while your peers in the Connecticut Valley cultivated cigar tobacco.

The problem was, if you and your family continued to live in rural areas in the East, your income began to decline. But if you moved to the Midwest or to the thriving industrial cities of the East, you could earn more money working in the factories.[8]

Social Changes

Before 19th-century America, if you weren't working in agriculture, you probably performed some kind of skilled trade. In the mid-1800s, your sons likely left home when they were about 22.5 years old, while your daughters left when they were around 20. However, if you sent your children off to be apprentices in one trade or another, they typically left home when they were much younger.

According to a study of rural Maryland, nearly 20 percent of white males aged 15–20 apprenticed in 1800, but dropped to less than 1 percent by 1860. However, with the advent of industrial production, it was hard to find apprenticeships. Some craftsmen moved up to the middle class by becoming factory managers, even owners.[9]

Consequently, if you lived in the North from 1815 to 1860, you might have been part of the small, well-to-do group of people who controlled a large portion of the economy. More likely, you were a member of the working poor, which included immigrants who owned nothing, or very little. Many skilled workers continued to be wage-earners with little hope for advancement. Even though you were making more money you had few, if any, opportunities to move up socially.[10]

Additionally, more than five million immigrants arrived in the United States from 1820 to 1860. Unfortunately, what the immigrants found when they arrived in the big cities wasn't all good: poverty, disease, and crime. Factory workers lived in tenement buildings that rapidly declined into slums. Living conditions in general were appalling as slums were breeding grounds for smallpox, tuberculosis, cholera, typhoid, and many other diseases that thrived in unsanitary conditions.[11]

Layoffs were so common, you found yourself out of work more times than you could count and that contributed to your overall feeling of uncertainty. To make matters worse, child labor was rampant. Child labor was widespread in agriculture and industry in the United States during the First Industrial Revolution. In the colonial period (1492–1763) and into the 1800s, you typically required your children to work.[12]

Initially, your children worked on farms; as they grew older, you gradually moved them into jobs that required greater strength and skills, such as carpentry and some metal work, to make things for the farm and to keep property in repair. However, even though your children were helping out on the farm, you really weren't making any more money.

Within each region, families in different life-cycle stages earned revenues in almost exactly the same manner. At every life-cycle stage, farm-owning families in the Midwest, for example, earned approximately 30 percent of their gross farm revenue from growing cereal crops; 29 percent from dairy, poultry, and market gardens; 22 percent from land and capital improvements; and 15 percent from hay and livestock.[13]

In fact, you actually lost money for every child under 7 you had working on your farm, likely because their mother had to care for them and couldn't

"This is cow country, pal, and we're not real big on innovation."

Figure 1.1. Source: ©Cartoon Resource.

work as much. If your children were aged 7–12, you earned about $16 more per year—7 percent of the income that you, as a typical adult male, would earn. If you had a teenage daughter working in the fields, she could boost your family's income by approximately $22 annually, while your teenage son could add $58 a year to your total income.[14] Since your children really weren't all that productive, you couldn't make a lot of money by putting them to work. The truth was that the cost of raising your children was usually more than the money they brought in.

As such, one of the reasons children were a great source of labor in many early industrial firms was because they didn't bring in much money working on their families' farms. In fact, in 1820, children 15 years and younger made up 23 percent of the Northeast' manufacturing labor force, which was undergoing industrialization then. Child labor was very common in textile factories. Children comprised 50 percent of the workforce in cotton mills with

16 or more employees, as well as 24 percent in paper mills and 41 percent of workers in wool mills.[15]

The use of child labor in manufacturing began to decline in 1840. However, many textile manufacturers hired entire families and—despite the decline in the use of child labor—continued to be an important part of this industry until the early 20th century.[16]

Major Breakthroughs Related to Employment

If you were a farmer, retailer, or professional in these flourishing agricultural areas, you amassed wealth that became available for other economic sectors, particularly manufacturing. As a factory owner or an owner of a small workshop, you accumulated money so you could produce a wide range of goods such as boards, boxes, utensils, building hardware, furniture, and wagons—products that were in demand in agricultural areas. This enabled a wide availability of cheap commodities, "which engendered a consumer culture that marked the end of many rural Americans' subsistence lifestyle."[17]

As your business became more productive, you enlarged your market area, although this didn't account for all of the industrial development then. Certain products, such as shoes, tinware, buttons, and cotton textiles, were in high demand by residents of prosperous agricultural areas as well as residents of large cities. These products were high value because it didn't cost much to ship them long distances. In addition, savvy entrepreneurs developed production methods and marketing approaches to sell these goods in large market areas, including New England and the Mid-Atlantic region of the country.[18]

Shoes and Tinware

Businessmen in Massachusetts became involved with developing an integrated shoe production complex based on dividing work among shops. Other entrepreneurs established marketing units consisting of wholesalers, mainly in Boston, who sold shoes throughout New England, Mid-Atlantic, and the South, especially to slave plantations. Entrepreneurs in Connecticut were into tinware, plated ware, buttons, and wooden clocks—goods that could be manufactured in small workshops. However, dividing the work among various shops wasn't as important as organized production within each shop.[19]

Firms producing shoes in Massachusetts as well as the Connecticut firms manufacturing tinware and associated goods tended to cluster in small subregions of their respective states. This enabled them to share information about production techniques as well as the specialized skills that they developed. Workers moving among the shops communicated this knowledge.

A marketing system of peddlers emerged in tinware who first sold their wares throughout Connecticut. Ultimately, they traveled to the rest of New England and the Mid-Atlantic peddling their goods.[20] If your workshop produced other types of light, high-value goods, you were able to take advantage of the peddler distribution system to increase your market areas. Initially, these peddlers only worked part of the year, but as market demand increased and the supply of goods grew, peddlers traveled farther and worked for longer periods of the year.

Like a number of factories and mills that sprang up in the next few decades, Slater's mill was powered by steam, which initially meant industrial development was confined to the Northeast. But these industries also facilitated the development of transportation systems such as canals and railroads that promoted commerce and trade.[21] If you were part of American society during the 19th century, particularly after the War of 1812, you experienced some big changes.

During these years, you witnessed rapid economic and territorial expansion as well as the extension of democratic politics. You were part of the first labor and reform movements. You saw the growth of cities and industries, and deepening conflicts that would bring the country to the verge of civil war. If you were a woman, you saw your role and your status change dramatically.[22]

Cotton Textiles

In 1790, there were fewer than 60,000 free African Americans. By 1810, that number rose to over 186,000. In many New England cities and towns, free African-Americans could vote, send their children to public schools, own land and businesses, establish churches, promote education, founded mutual aid societies, developed print culture, and voted.

Still, the slave population continued to grow—from less than 700,000 in 1790 to more than 1.5 million by 1820. The growth of abolition in the North and the rise in slavery in the South continued to divide the two regions.[23] This process was driven by cotton. Although it was becoming less profitable for farmers to maintain slaves in tobacco planting areas such as Virginia, the growth of the cotton industry increased the demand for slaves, and cotton farmers were able to invest their new profits in acquiring new slaves.[24]

Come early 19th century, states north of the Mason-Dixon Line attempted to abolish slavery. Vermont included abolition as a provision of its 1777 state constitution. The Emancipation Act of 1780 in Pennsylvania specified freed children serve a 28-year indenture term. In 1804, New Jersey became the last of the northern states to gradually emancipate slaves. Many states in the North said they would only liberate future children born to women who were slaves. These laws also stipulated these children remain in indentured servitude to their mothers' masters to compensate slaveholders for losses.[25]

The cotton textile industry was also good if you were an entrepreneur, but not so good if you were a woman working long hours for very little pay. Much like other manufacturers who enlarged their market areas throughout the East before 1820, the cotton manufacturing business was set up in prosperous agricultural areas.

This made sense because if you wanted your company to be successful, you needed a lot of money, good technical skills, and access to nearby markets to sell. However, the process involved in manufacturing cotton textiles was different than approaches involved with shoes or small metal and wooden products.[26]

From the beginning, processes to manufacture cotton textiles included the use of textile machinery, at first spinning machines to make yarn, then after 1815, weaving machines and other mechanical equipment. That meant you had to hire very skilled mechanics to build and maintain those machines. In addition, because it took more money to operate cotton mills than manufacturing shoes and small goods, you looked to merchant wholesalers, wealthy retailers, professionals, mill owners, and others to help fund your factory.[27]

If you were a top cotton textile manufacturer in the 1790s, you were in New England, particularly Rhode Island. Merchants in Providence, Rhode Island, funded early successful cotton spinning mills, drawing on the talents of Samuel Slater. Slater trained many textile mechanics and encouraged investors in various parts of Rhode Island, Connecticut, Massachusetts, New Hampshire, and New York to build mills.[28]

Power-loom weaving began to be commercially feasible between 1815 and 1820, led by firms in Rhode Island and Massachusetts. A merchant

**"Ah ha, here's your problem.
You're trying to make a living as a farmer."**

Figure 1.2. Source: ©Cartoon Resource.

living in Boston spent time developing business plans targeting large-scale, integrated cotton textile manufacturing, with marketing and sales housed in separate firms. After 1820, the growth of the cotton textile industry increased because entrepreneurs were very successful at lowering production costs.[29]

By the middle of the 1800s, the number of people working in textile mills had grown to 85,000, producing cloth goods valued at $68 million annually. Cotton and woolen textile mills were the nation's leading industrial employers during this time.[30]

The Railroad

John Stevens received the first railroad charter in North America in 1815 and was instrumental in building the first railway systems for steam locomotives. The first American-built steam locomotive operated on a common-carrier railroad in 1830. After that, railroads began transporting freight back and forth between the East Coast and Great Lakes, paving the way for a network of rail lines that spanned relatively short distances.

If you were a businessman, the growth of rail lines helped you get rich, and you soon began dreaming of a railroad that would stretch from coast to coast so you could reap some of the riches the West had to offer.[31]

Women and the First Industrial Revolution in the United States

One of the unintended consequences of technological change during the First Industrial Revolution was the greater role for women in the labor force, politics, and reform activities. For example, adopting the power loom enabled companies to conduct all the steps in cloth manufacturing within the mill. This change also resulted in a change in the labor force.[32]

Because fairly tall workers were needed to run the power looms and dressing frames, companies couldn't use children the way they had for mills in southern New England. Consequently, from the beginning, the Boston Manufacturing Company in Waltham, Massachusetts, recruited young, single women from the state's rural areas to work in factories. The company built boardinghouses to accommodate them. To entice women to leave home to go work in the city, managers offered monthly cash wages.[33]

From 1830 to 1860, women remained a key labor force for the growing mill industry. Mill owners and executives hired recruiters to travel throughout northern New England to bring suitable young women to work in their mills. They typically earned between $3.00 and $3.50 a week, much higher than they could have earned working on farms in their hometowns. Since they came from farmer families and were able to maintain modest livings, they didn't decide to look for work in the mills because they were poor. Rather they wanted to be independent and self-supporting.[34]

In addition, these women saved money to help their families and for their weddings. They achieved a measure of economic and social independence they wouldn't have if they continued living with their parents. This brought about significant cultural changes. Some people worried working in the mills made women less fit for marriage because they had become urbanized. They also worried women would no longer be satisfied with the country life of their parents.[35]

Like many women who worked in the mills, they likely married artisans or other urban workers and settled in New England's growing cities rather than move back to farms. In 1858, one writer complained that young working women no longer wanted to live on the farm—a perception based on reality as only with about a third of marrying farmers or farm laborers. About a quarter of those who married lived in their mill towns for the rest of their lives.[36]

Women also became involved in reform movements of the antebellum decades. In the 1830s and 1840s there were labor protests in Lowell, Massachusetts, and other New England mill towns. As the antislavery movement was strong in Lowell, many mill women decided to send several petitions to Washington opposing slavery in the District of Columbia and opposing war with Mexico, which people feared would cause slavery to expand into the Southwest.[37]

Women participated in women's rights conventions that continued to be held; the first one took place in Seneca Falls, New York, in July 1848. Experiences of women who worked in mills brought women's work out of the home and provided a collective experience supporting participation for broader social reform.[38]

Women became involved in causes of the time: antislavery, labor reform, peace, moral reform, prison reform, and women's rights. In addition, like working men during this time, they initially drew on republican traditions to defend their rights and interests. Ultimately, women justified their concerns for social justice on religious and rationalist grounds. They began to oppose the growing inequality they saw in American society and demanded greater rights and rewards for themselves.[39]

The Role of Education

During the First Industrial Revolution, education was not the main focus in America. People spent most of their time working on farms or factory lines. But after the American Revolution, priorities gradually began to encompass education. Congress wrote legislation that set aside enough land in every township for schools.

Even so, after the 1803 Louisiana Purchase increased the nation's territory, and commerce was important economically, interest in the classical lives of Romans and Greeks declined nationally, with grammar schools becoming less dominant.[40] Tax-supported public education triumphed during 1825–1850. Although it lagged in the South, laborers, who wielded increasing influence, demanded instruction for their children.

The little red schoolhouse consisting of one room, one stove, one teacher, and often eight grades became prominent but they were only open a few months of the year. And if you were a schoolteacher—most were men during this time—you were too often not well-educated, short-tempered, overworked, and underpaid.[41]

Horace Mann, a Massachusetts legislator who became secretary of the Massachusetts Board of Education, knew reform was essential. He campaigned effectively for more and better schoolhouses, longer school terms, higher pay for teachers, and an expanded curriculum. Other states soon followed Mann's lead, but despite these improvements, education was still an expensive luxury for many communities.

Better textbooks, particularly those of Noah Webster, a Yale-educated Connecticut Yankee known as the "Schoolmaster of the Republic," helped advance education. His reading lessons used by millions of children in the 19th century were created in part to promote patriotism. Webster spent 20 years writing his dictionary published in 1828, thus standardizing the American language.[42]

William H. McGuffey, a teacher-preacher from Ohio, published 1–6 grade readers, widely used as textbooks from mid-1800s to mid-1900s. McGuffey's Readers taught students about morality, patriotism, and idealism.[43]

In the late 1790s, Benjamin Rush from Pennsylvania, a signer of the Declaration of Independence, pushed for formal instruction for girls because he felt they were guardians of society's morality. Soon industrialization changed familiar social roles. If you were a woman, you began replacing male schoolteachers in larger cities in the 19th century. By 1818, you were teaching in Boston primary schools that only employed female teachers.[44]

You were lucky you lived in urban areas in the East. Across the country, attempts to educate women were not widespread. Many religious denominations, such as the German Reformed Church, didn't want their daughters to go to school. Even people who advocated for education for girls in the 19th century were really talking about "finishing schools" for females to learn social graces they'd be able to teach to their sons.[45]

Higher Education

Higher education was emerging with many small, denominational, liberal arts colleges springing up in the South and West. Often, they weren't up to par academically. They were established to satisfy local pride rather than advance the cause of learning. As an adult, you often satisfied your quest for knowledge at private subscription libraries or, increasingly, at tax-supported libraries (traveling lecturers helped bring learning to the people through lyceum lecture associations).[46]

By the time they joined the Union, the New England and Mid-Atlantic states were already home to private colleges such as: Harvard, founded in 1636; Yale, in Connecticut (1701); Princeton, in New Jersey (1746); Columbia, in New York (1754); University of Pennsylvania (1749); Brown, in Rhode Island (1764); Dartmouth, in New Hampshire (1769); and Bowdoin, in Maine (1794).

Although Vermont didn't have a private college when it became a state in 1791, it was the only state among nine in the Northeast to set up a state-funded and state-controlled university before the Civil War. The University of Vermont was founded in 1791 several years before Middlebury College (the first private institution in the state, established in 1800).[47]

The first state-supported universities sprang up in the South, beginning with the University of Georgia in 1785, followed by the University of North Carolina in 1789. Federal land grants enabled these institutions to flourish. The University of Virginia in 1816 received its state charter under a plan crafted by Thomas Jefferson, opening in 1825. Jefferson designed the architecture and dedicated the university, which emphasized modern languages and sciences, to freedom from religious or political constraints. Then, state colleges and universities were established to turn out people who could teach at elementary (or common) and secondary (or grammar) schools.[48]

If you were a woman in the early decades of the 19th century, you weren't encouraged to attend college because, according to societal norms, your place was in the home and it was more important for you to learn needlecraft than algebra. People thought learning would hurt your feminine brain, make you ill and unfit for marriage. In the 1820s, secondary schools for women finally began to gain some respectability, thanks in part to Emma Willard who established Troy Female Seminary in 1821. Oberlin College in 1837 shocked traditionalists when it opened its doors to women and men.

The Role of Corporations

For hundreds of years corporations have been key institutions of the American economy in significantly contributing to growth. Then, as today, people questioned whether the U.S. government was a government of the people or a government "of the corporations, by the corporations, and for the corporations." These fears existed in the 1790s, when the United States began to lead the world in developing corporations as the most dynamic form of modern business. These fears surfaced again during the financial and economic crises of the late 1830s and early 1840s, after state legislatures had established thousands of corporations.[49]

Americans have always had mixed feelings about corporations. Investors find a corporation with limited liability and longevity attractive that they pool their monies, receiving in return shares of the company to trade. "Pooling of capital makes possible large, long-term investments that can achieve economies of scale and scope in the production and distribution of goods and services that are beyond the capabilities of sole proprietorships and partnerships."[50]

However, inherent in these corporations were conflicting goals. For example, were corporations managed in the interests of shareholders? Or were corporate managers acting in their own self-interests? Did corporate managers take into account the interests of employees, customers, suppliers, lenders, and the administrations that made the corporation possible?[51] These problems of conflicting corporate goals have existed since American corporations were established.

The United States led the world in modern corporate development from 1790 to 1860, with 22,419 business corporations receiving charters under special legislative acts. The number of corporations in the United States far exceeded those in any other country—maybe even all countries combined—during that time.[52]

Most early American corporations were small compared to those established later. The largest corporations were insurance companies and banks, joined later by manufacturers and railroads.[53]

Legislative chartering allowed customization for each corporation in specifying its powers, responsibilities, including those to community, and provisions for basic governance.[54] Most charters had set terms of years, to be renewed periodically as a hedge against corporate malfeasance. When it came to electing directors as well as in other corporate matters, shareholders' rules varied; it was not always the one vote per share rule that favored large-block shareholders.[55] "Legislative chartering could easily be corrupted, however, with incumbent corporations using money and influence to defeat charters for potential competitors, and would-be corporations using the same tools to gain charters."[56] The laws of general incorporation were introduced in the years leading up to the Civil War to avoid corruption involved in legislative chartering and what was thought to be close relationships between corporations and the states.

Access to corporations became more open, which was good for society. However, state oversight of the creation and monitoring of corporations was reduced. Consequently, corporate governance suffered.[57]

What Happened Next?

As the First Industrial Revolution in the United States gave way to the Second Industrial Revolution, many people began to suffer economic insecurities as they lived through the depressions of the 1870s and 1890s. Large numbers of individuals lost their jobs or had their earnings reduced. Factory workers worked long hours in extremely dangerous working conditions with long hours for low wages. Those unfortunate to be hurt on the job weren't compensated. When they retired, they didn't receive pensions to help them live out their golden years.[58]

During this time, if you wanted to be economically independent, you had to have a technical skill, rather than just work in your own shop. If you were lucky to be a skilled worker, you received high wages in industrial work and you oversaw a great deal of the production process. This was labeled "progress" by proponents, but if you worked on the floor in a factory, you knew this economic independence came at a price.[59]

Trailblazing Leaders of the First Industrial Revolution

There were many individuals who contributed to the First Industrial Revolution in the United States, thus enabling career development, including:

- Eli Whitney invented the cotton gin in 1794, which quickly and easily separated cotton fibers from seeds, with greater productivity than manual cotton separation.[60]
- Robert Fulton, with Robert Livingston, built the North River Steamboat (later known as the Clermont), the first commercially successful steamboat in 1807. The steamboat carried passengers between New York City and upstream to the state capital Albany. The Clermont was able to make the 150-mile trip in 32 hours.[61]
- Cyrus McCormick invented the mechanical reaper in 1831, enabling farmers to harvest crops mechanically, rapidly, and with fewer workers.[62]
- Hiram Moore invented the first combine harvester in 1834, developed to save time and money by enabling farmers to harvest crops without manual labor.[63]
- John Deere invented the first commercially successful lightweight plow with a steel cutting edge in 1837, ideal for tough soils of the Midwest.[64]
- Margaret Fuller (1810–1850) was a leading proponent of women's rights and first female editor of the *New York Tribune*; she wrote influential articles about women's rights and progressive social policies.[65]
- Susan B. Anthony (1820–1906), a campaigner for civil rights and women's suffrage, was a highly influential activist who secured for women the right to vote.[66]

Notes

1. http://www.ushistory.org/us/22a.asp.
2. http://www.pbs.org/wgbh/theymadeamerica/whomade/slater_hi.html.
3. http://www.americanyawp.com/text/08-the-market-revolution/.
4. Ibid.
5. http://ic.galegroup.com/ic/suic/ReferenceDetailsPage/ReferenceDetailsWindow?zid=53d fc629075ed73f7b4ce227040896c3&action=2&catId=GALE%7C00000000MNX3 &documentId=GALE%7CEJ3048500105&source=Bookmark&u=cps1620&jsid=8b 346d6c8312e2ccce710fd1c7aea7ee.
6. https://eh.net/encyclopedia/the-roots-of-american-industrialization-1790-1860/.

7. http://www.americanyawp.com/text/08-the-market-revolution/.

8. https://eh.net/encyclopedia/the-roots-of-american-industrialization-1790-1860/.

9. https://eh.net/encyclopedia/child-labor-in-the-united-states/.

10. https://eh.net/encyclopedia/the-roots-of-american-industrialization-1790-1860/.

11. http://www.americanyawp.com/text/08-the-market-revolution/.

12. https://eh.net/encyclopedia/child-labor-in-the-united-states/.

13. Ibid.

14. Ibid.

15. Ibid.

16. Ibid.

17. http://education.seattlepi.com/extent-did-industrial-revolution-change-american-social-economic-political-life-6960.html.

18. Ibid.

19. Ibid.

20. Ibid.

21. http://www.loc.gov/teachers/classroommaterials/primarysourcesets/industrial-revolution/pdf/teacher_guide.pdf.

22. http://www.digitalhistory.uh.edu/era.cfm?eraid=5.

23. http://www.americanyawp.com/text/08-the-market-revolution/.

24. Ibid.

25. Ibid.

26. https://eh.net/encyclopedia/the-roots-of-american-industrialization-1790-1860/.

27. Ibid.

28. Ibid.

29. Ibid.

30. https://www.gilderlehrman.org/history-by-era/age-jackson/essays/women-and-early-industrial-revolution-united-states.

31. http://ic.galegroup.com/ic/suic/ReferenceDetailsPage/ReferenceDetailsWindow?zid=53dfc629075ed73f7b4ce227040896c3&action=2&catId=GALE%7C00000000MNX3&documentId=GALE%7CEJ3048500105&userGroupName=cps1620&jsid=af71e044e514e9123e23ec660aa19873.

32. https://www.gilderlehrman.org/history-by-era/age-jackson/essays/women-and-early-industrial-revolution-united-states.

33. Ibid.

34. Ibid.

35. Ibid.

36. Ibid.

37. Ibid.

38. Ibid.

39. Ibid.

40. http://education.stateuniversity.com/pages/1627/United-States-HISTORY-BACKGROUND.html.

41. https://www.apstudynotes.org/us-history/outlines/chapter-15-the-ferment-of-reform-and-culture-1790-1860/.

42. Ibid.
43. Ibid.
44. http://education.stateuniversity.com/pages/1627/United-States-HISTORY-BACK
GROUND.html.
45. Ibid.
46. https://www.apstudynotes.org/us-history/outlines/chapter-15-the-ferment-of-reform-and-culture-1790-1860/.
47. https://www.apstudynotes.org/us-history/outlines/chapter-15-the-ferment-of-reform-and-culture-1790-1860/.
48. https://www.apstudynotes.org/us-history/outlines/chapter-15-the-ferment-of-reform-and-culture-1790-1860/.
49. https://www.amacad.org/content/publications/pubContent.aspx?d=1053.
50. Ibid.
51. Ibid.
52. Ibid.
53. Ibid.
54. Ibid.
55. Ibid.
56. Ibid.
57. Ibid.
58. http://ushistoryscene.com/article/second-industrial-revolution/.
59. Ibid.
60. http://www.history.com/topics/inventions/cotton-gin-and-eli-whitney.
61. https://en.wikipedia.org/wiki/Robert_Fulton.
62. http://study.com/academy/lesson/mechanical-reaper-invention-impact-facts.html.
63. https://prezi.com/6cog1z4rqqjt/the-first-combine-was-made-by-hiram-moore-in-the-us-in-1834/.
64. https://en.wikipedia.org/wiki/John_Deere_(inventor).
65. https://www.biography.com/people/margaret-fuller-9303889.
66. https://www.biography.com/people/susan-b-anthony-194905.

· 2 ·

THE SECOND INDUSTRIAL REVOLUTION

The Second Industrial Revolution (1870–1914) made America the world's leading industrial power. By 1913, the United States produced one-third of the world's output, besting the combined productivity of the United Kingdom, France, and Germany.[1] It was a great leap forward for technological and social progress—so soon after the Civil War (1861–1865). Factors that enabled this leap forward included an abundance of natural resources (coal, oil, iron), large and cheap labor supplies, newer sources of power (electricity), railroads, American inventors and inventions (long distance communications with Alexander Graham Bell's telephone in 1876; Thomas Edison's light bulb in 1879, which allowed factory work to continue at night), and strong government policies.

Before the 19th century, if you weren't working on your family's farm, you performed some type of skilled trade. But the advent of industrialization meant there was less need for apprenticeships or craftsmen. There was also less need for commoditized labor; cheap commodities became readily available as the Second Industrial Revolution progressed, effectively ending the subsistence lifestyles of American farmers.[2]

This period fueled mass advancements in agriculture, manufacturing, and transportation. If you were a farmer or owned a manufacturing company,

"Success has changed you."

Figure 2.1. Source: ©Cartoon Resource.

advances in technology made it easier for you to grow more crops and produce or make more goods to sell. However, although you enjoyed a higher standard of living than citizens in the past, many of your peers were unemployed because machines had taken over their jobs.[3]

Still, as costs of manufacturing goods fell, so did prices, resulting in increased demand and productivity. Additionally, the large numbers of immigrants entering the United States brought new ideas and inventions that spread rapidly. These developments made huge contributions to the Second Industrial Revolution in the United States and abroad, in providing new ways of doing things that made life easier and allowed more people to create new products, and as well introducing new lifestyles away from farms.[4]

Factory owners took full advantage of harnessing human labor, increasing from 2.4 million to 10 million workers. From 1880 to 1920, employment in the manufacturing sector grew more than twice as fast as other industries. However, as a factory worker, you soon realized your employer didn't pay much attention to your rights as an employee.[5]

In 1880, 5 million people, including immigrants, women, and children, who could be paid less than men for the same work simultaneously, toiled together in factories. In 1900, an American male factory worker made about $483 a year, or $1.55 per day; a male immigrant earned slightly less. Women were paid half the rate of an American male, with children typically receiving a third.[6]

If you lived on a farm, you likely moved to the city in search of work and a better life. But you were probably disappointed because things were not as easy as you thought they'd be. That's because you didn't have the knowledge or the skills necessary to do your job the "right way." For instance, if you worked on a factory assembly line, you probably performed a task that took less than a minute to complete. However, you often didn't know much about how your work fit in with the total operation. To pass the time, you introduced variety into your work and/or changed the way you did your job. But doing that often contributed to already dangerous working conditions. Consequently, between 1880 and 1900 an average of 35,000 of your peers died every year in factory and mine accidents, the highest rate in the industrial world.[7]

From 1870 to 1890, the economy grew significantly and living standards improved greatly as the price of goods fell because of increases in productivity. However, unemployment also increased, disrupting commerce and industry. As a result, if you were a factory worker, you were likely displaced by machines.[8]

Railroads enabled raw materials and goods including agricultural produce to be transported more economically. If farms in areas connected to major markets via the railroads failed to produce crops, people didn't starve because food could still be shipped over the rails. But that was bad news if you were a farmer whose livelihood was on the line.[9]

You were thus constantly worried about supporting yourself and your family. Economic depressions of the 1870s and the 1890s put millions of people out of work, or caused paychecks to be reduced. If you were a worker during the Second Industrial Revolution, you most likely toiled in very poor conditions and were treated very badly.

As an American worker during the 1870s and 1880s, you probably joined your peers to form national labor unions, to more effectively negotiate with big corporations. You may have even joined the Knights of Labor, one of the most important early U.S. labor organizations. This union organized workers into one big brotherhood, rather than separate unions of workers working in a certain industry or had a common skill.[10]

Ultimately, the Knights became a national organization that welcomed workers of every kind, no matter their skills, sex, nationality, or race—well, almost all workers. You could forget about joining if you were a banker, gambler, lawyer, or saloonkeeper.

In 1885, the Knights reportedly had 700,000 members, and predominantly Catholic. Even though the union didn't approve of strikes to settle labor disputes, they won major victories against the Union Pacific railroad in 1884 and the Wabash railroad in 1885.[11] The Knights also campaigned for an eight-hour workday, abolishment of child labor, better factory safety, equal pay for men and women, and compensation for injuries suffered on the job. Rather than paying wages to employees, the Knights favored workshops and stores run as cooperatives. The Knights held the first Labor Day celebration in 1882.[12]

As a worker, you likely agreed with what the Knights stood for because you were looking to better your own working conditions. However, after at least eight people were killed including seven policemen by a bomb during a demonstration in Chicago's Haymarket Square in 1886, the Knights declined rapidly. The demonstration protested the slayings of two workers during a strike. Eight radical labor activists were convicted for this bombing, although without not much evidence. Even so, people blamed the riot on labor "radicalism," which in turned caused the public to condemn the Knights.[13]

The Knights were replaced by the American Federation of Labor which, unlike the Knights, united skilled craftsmen and their unions committed to "bread-and-butter" unionism. You probably gravitated to this union because it sought to increase your wages, reduce your working hours, and improve your working conditions.[14]

In 1905, the union of Industrial Workers of the World (iww.org) was founded to create safe and manageable working conditions. The goal of this and other unions was to ensure workplaces benefited workers and communities, not just bosses and executives.

In 1908, the Federal Employers Liability Act was enacted. This Act protected you if you were a railroad worker injured on the job and if it was determined that the railroad was at least partly legally negligent.[15]

Railroads and Their Impact

Rail companies were instrumental in opening up America's vast interior and natural resources for prospecting, further developing commerce and industries with related industries such as mining, even hospitality. English immigrant Fred Harvey founded this country's first restaurant chain in 1876 with "Harvey Houses" in tandem with the railroads. Harvey's secret sauce was introducing

"I want a fair day's wage
for a fair day's work."

Figure 2.2. Source: ©Cartoon Resource.

fresh food and quality service for rail travelers at his "eating houses" built alongside rail lines—and in dining cars on the Atchison, Topeka, and Santa Fe Railway (aka ATSF or the "Santa Fe"). Over five thousand "Harvey Girls" staffed these eateries and were expected to serve out at least one full year before leaving or getting married.[16]

The Santa Fe pioneered intermodal freight transportation.[17] Meaning, ATSF's rail connections included bus lines to ferry you out from railway stations to destinations not served by rail—including tugboat ferry services in the Bay Area. So, if you could afford it, you traveled from the Midwest to San Francisco through the exotic American Southwest by rail on the Santa Fe—assured of great rail hospitality with quality food, great service, and clean lodging all along the way.

However, thousands more who were not well-heeled tourists but had to work the rail systems were not so fortunate. The Great Railroad Strike of 1877 brought to light wretched conditions rail workers had to suffer. Baltimore and Ohio Railroad (B&O) workers destroyed and burned down rail engines and cars on July 14 in Martinsburg, West Virginia—after wages were cut a third time that year. This started a chain reaction, causing the first workers' strike in the United States, inciting more destruction of rail property and buildings through New York, Pennsylvania, Illinois, and Missouri. At that time, railroads were the second largest employers outside agriculture. It ended 45 days later with federal intervention. In 1884, B&O offered the first worker pension plan by a major employer.[18]

Impact on Women

As a woman, the Second Industrial Revolution brought both positive and negative consequences to you. During this time, many young men moved from the country to the city looking for work in shipyards, factories, and offices because farm jobs where their parents and grandparents had worked had dried up. Having been controlled by your family for so long, you yearned for and began living an independent life. As a single young woman you were also searching for opportunities. You wanted to experience life on your own in the big city. You didn't want to be locked into the expectation you'd marry a neighbor boy and work his farm as women in your family had done previously.[19]

But if you decided not to work in a factory, you may have found work as a teacher, nurse, or housekeeper. Many women earned a living with their sewing skills doing piecework at home and making clothes. You became friends with your fellow workers and other women who lived in your all-female boarding house. On your own for the first time, you had the freedom to explore everything your new environment offered. You were even able to pursue the same type of nighttime and weekend fun activities that were previously only open to men.[20]

However, working conditions for "women's work" were so dismal you faced poor pay and negligent safety conditions. You could have gone on strike with other women, as did some women a year before their tragic Triangle Fire on March 25, 1911 where 123 women and 23 men lost their lives.[21]

You then started getting more involved in your political rights and for others. As you participated in workers' rights movements, you organized your own unions and stood shoulder-to-shoulder with men fighting for higher wages, better conditions, and shorter working hours.

You confused your relatives at home, who didn't think this was a good thing. They still believed women weren't supposed to have their own thoughts, ideas, or ambitions, but were supposed to stay home quietly doing their embroidery, agreeing with their husbands' conversations, and laughing at their children's antics.[22]

However, the wheels of change had started churning, gathering more momentum. Women's rights activists like Susan B. Anthony and Elizabeth Cady Stanton (both were also abolitionists) championed women's rights. Stanton and Lucretia Mott organized the first women's rights convention in the summer of 1848 in Seneca Falls, New York, attracting 240 attendees. One hundred delegates (68 women and 32 men) signed a "Declaration of Sentiments" modeled after the Declaration of Independence declaring women and men as equal citizens with the right to vote.[23]

Anthony and Stanton founded the National Woman Suffrage Association in 1869, and coedited three volumes of the six-volume History of Woman Suffrage (1881–1922). They published the weekly The Revolution, lobbying for women's equal rights. Both women collaborated in pioneering women's political and social rights. In 1866, they formed the American Equal Rights Association (ERA) to secure equal rights for all Americans regardless of race, color, or sex.[24]

Anthony, arrested for voting illegally in the 1872 presidential election, was fined $100, but she never paid it. Fourteen years after her passing, the 19th Amendment in 1920 accorded women voting rights. Today, Susan B. Anthony is memorialized with the first dollar coin in honor of a woman minted by the U.S. Treasury; it came out in 1979 and continues circulating its significant groundbreaking message for equal rights.[25]

In another breakthrough, Victoria Claflin Woodhull made her mark as the first woman candidate running for the U.S. presidential office in 1872, with an African-American running mate, abolitionist Frederick Douglass. An ardent women's rights activist, she campaigned for labor rights and "free love" (meaning the freedom to marry, divorce, and have children without government interference). With her sister Tennessee Claflin, both became the first women to own and operate a Wall Street brokerage firm.[26]

The Growth of Big Business

After the Civil War, a new economy emerged in the United States fueled by steam-powered manufacturing, railroads, electric motor, internal combustion engine, and the practical application of chemistry. This new economy depended on raw materials from around the world, with companies selling goods in global markets.

Victoria Claflin Woodhull for President 1872.

Figure 2.3. Source: ©Cartoon Resource.

The value of American manufacturing increased from $3 billion to $13 billion, from 1869 to 1910. For instance, in 1870, the steel industry produced 68,000 tons and in 1890, 4.2 million tons—thanks to the modern corporation.[27]

Factories had become more mechanized, hence producing more goods. By the beginning of the 20th century, a few giant corporations dominated America's major industries, for example, banking, manufacturing, meatpacking, oil refining, railroads, and steel.[28]

Along with the rise in big business came a new class of millionaires. At the start of the Civil War, there were only 400 millionaires in the United States, but that number increased to 4,047 by 1892. Many positive developments associated with the growth of the modern corporation included rapidly increasing productivity due to mechanization, standardization, and economies of scale. As an urban worker between 1890 and 1929, you worked one less day per week and brought home three times more pay. You and your family enjoyed comforts and conveniences you never imagined before 1890.[29]

By 1929, you most likely had electricity, indoor plumbing, a refrigerator, and an automobile. You probably listened to your favorite programs on the radio, played your favorite records on your phonograph—and your life expectancy increased by 20 years.

In 1888, Charles E. Perkins, president of the Chicago, Burlington, and Quincy Railroad, exhorted, "Have not the great merchants, great manufacturers, great inventors, done more for the world than preachers and philanthropists? Can there be any doubt that cheapening the cost of necessaries and conveniences of life is the most powerful agent of civilization and progress?"[30]

Yet during this time, you were also anxious about continuing to make a living with large businesses accused of abusing workers, corrupting the political process, and manufacturing shoddy, unsafe products. You and your peers were afraid businesses were using their power to fix prices and influence government decision-making.[31]

During the Second Industrial Revolution, businesses grew bigger because:

- The shift from water-powered to coal-powered factories enabled manufacturers to build plants closer to markets and suppliers.
- Improvements in transportation meant companies could distribute products to regional and national markets.
- The creation of new financial institutions such as commercial banks, stock market, and investment houses increased the availability of investment capital.

However, the modern corporation was largely the result of economic instability, with competition among businesses increasing greatly during the late 19th century.[32]

The Corporate Revolution

During the late 1800s, businesses in America radically transformed the way they were structured and operated. Before the 1870s, the typical business was financed by one person or by several people forming a partnership. Most businesses were owned and built by a wealthy few. In the 1880s, the average factory had less than $1,800 investment and the largest textile factories represented less than $1 million in investment.[33]

In 1862, John D. Rockefeller from Cleveland, Ohio, joined with two partners to establish an oil-refining company, ultimately becoming Standard Oil. During the 1870s and 1880s, Rockefeller expanded and drove some oil refineries out of business while buying out a number of others.[34] By 1878, Standard Oil Co. was worth $600 million.[35]

"The oil business is mine." John D. Rockefeller

Figure 2.4. Source: ©Cartoon Resource.

As businesses continued to grow, new bureaucratic hierarchies were necessary. Increasingly, the success of a business depended on central coordination. Therefore, businesses created formal administrative structures, such as purchasing and accounting departments. They required workers who had academic skills in writing and mathematics. With this "managerial revolution" came a "new middle class" consisting of white-collar workers in corporations, rather than the "older middle" made up of farmers, shopkeepers, and independent professionals.[36] As corporations expanded, they opened offices in various U.S. cities. Before the 1880s, a company typically operated from one office or factory in one town. By 1900, General Electric had plants in 23 cities.

Additionally, these new corporations also engaged in a number of operations. Pre-Civil War wholesalers, merchants, and manufacturers engaged in just one operation. However, by the late 19th century they had expanded their range of operations.[37] During the late 1800s, businesses grew vertically, that is, bringing together various phases of production and distribution. For example, a steel company would mine iron ore, transport to its mills, make steel, manufacture finished products, and ship products to wholesalers.

However, integrating horizontally meant a company expanded into related areas of business. For instance, an iron furnace company in the 1850s might produce a single product, such as cast iron implements or nails, but during the late 19th century, a company like U.S. Steel produced a vast array of metal goods.[38]

During the last third of the 19th century, the U.S. economy transformed significantly. After 30 years of large numbers of business failures and high unemployment, companies consolidated into increasingly larger economic units. However, this shift did not take place easily as working conditions in many factories were dreadful and labor conflicts intensified. Companies were accused of stock watering, price fixing, and other abuses. In the end, those abuses brought about political reaction and action. In the late 19th and the early 20th centuries, the federal government put new regulations in place to address problems exacerbated by corporate power.[39]

Previously, states had tried to regulate corporations tightly. A corporation was required to apply to its state legislature for a charter, which restricted how the company could operate, limited the amount of investment, and specified the length of the charter. Ultimately, legislatures found it too cumbersome to grant individual charters. Hence, state legislatures adopted general incorporation acts that allowed a business to incorporate and removed limits on capitalization.[40]

But it wasn't really clear what powers states had to regulate corporations or who was responsible if corporations broke the law, such as polluting the environment or fixing prices. In 1877, in *Munn v. Illinois*[41] the Supreme Court ruled state law setting maximum rates for grain storage was constitutional, which established the principle that states were empowered to regulate businesses for the public interest. Subsequently, the court backed off from this ruling regarding another case.

In an 1886 decision, *Santa Clara v. Southern Pacific Railroad Company*, the Supreme Court ruled that under the 14th Amendment corporations were guaranteed. In another 1886 decision, in the case of *Wabash, St. Louis & Pacific Railroad v. Illinois*, the court ruled the U.S. Congress had the exclusive right to regulate commerce between states and invalidated the attempts of some states to regulate business operations.[42]

In 1895, in *U.S. v. E.C. Knight*, the Supreme Court ruled the Sherman Antitrust Act adopted in 1890 didn't pertain to companies located within just one state. This decision severely weakened the federal government's ability to enforce antitrust laws.[43]

The Big Business Debate

During the late 19th century, there were great debates concerning big business. Americans debated such issues as:

- whether wealth came from exploitation or from patience, frugality, and virtue
- whether bigness was the result of conspiracy or of pressures of blind economic forces
- whether men of wealth and power were free to use their riches as they wished
- whether they should be taxed to support the public good[44]

Some people considered industry titans monopolists and profiteers who blocked success for competitors. Others said the captains of industry made all Americans better off because of their innovations in management, finance, and production.

Without a doubt in the late 1800s, these business lords were business innovators, whose technical, administrative, and financial skills enabled them to achieve economies of scale, eliminate waste, and bring order and stability to large sectors of the American economy.[45] In large part, the wealth of these business titans stemmed from innovations that radically transformed business practices. For example, John D. Rockefeller developed the oil tank-car; meat-packing mogul Gustavus Franklin Swift, Sr. developed the refrigerated rail car; and Montgomery Ward created the mail-order catalog.

But critics of big business accused these captains of industry of political corruption and bribing legislatures; and financial chicanery including cornering and watering stock. Critics attacked them for the abysmal ways they treated their employees, including long hours, cutting pay, lockouts, and suppressing trade unions.[46]

Those opposed to big businesses condemned corporation leaders for using cheap immigrant contract labor to undercut wages and defeat strikes as well as for imposing monopoly prices. Titans of industry were condemned as evil monopolists who stifled rivals via industrial espionage, railroad rebates and kickbacks, control of raw material supplies, and buying up rivals.[47] Many people compared these business leaders to the robber barons of the Middle Ages, who set up barriers across rivers, then forced boats to pay a toll to navigate the waterways.[48]

Transforming American Society

The Second Industrial Revolution transformed American society in many ways. For example:

- Urbanization increased quickly as people moved to cities to be closer to factories.
- Families were split apart with work shifting from home/farm to factories.
- Work was no longer seasonal; workers had to follow routine schedules.
- Driven by machines, the pace of work increased significantly.
- Workers' health declined due to unhealthy and dismal factory conditions.
- Work availability was unpredictable, increasing and decreasing with demands for goods.
- Many women who had moved to work in city factories lost their jobs with the introduction of machines. Cut off from family ties, many were forced into prostitution.
- Because they were unable to compete with lower costs of mass-produced goods, artisans and craftsmen lost their livelihoods.

- More people than ever before were able to afford factory-made goods.
- Close living and working conditions resulted in a sense of class consciousness among working people.

Takeaways

During the Second Industrial Revolution, imagination and progress thrived. New inventions enabled the manufacturing of new products, creating demands that caused a vicious cycle, driving some people to prosperity, while holding down others in poverty. Although inventors, scientists, and brilliant people never meant to cause such a chasm between the working class and the industrial machine era, it happened nonetheless.[49]

Machines displaced workers from performing harsh manual labor; workers became machine maintenance workers (similar to future industrial revolutions when people shifted from using computers as tools to harnessing them as co-partners for work). Increased automation meant productivity expanded exponentially, with urban workers in 1890–1929 paid three times more than previously.

Yet, similar to benefits accruing from major industrial revolutions, tragedies had to happen before worker improvements could be introduced, such as the 1911 Triangle Fire, after which finally work safety regulations were mandated in New York City. The Great Railroad Strike of 1877 started the first pension reform for workers by a major rail company, the B&O.

However, thanks to constantly emerging ideas and new inventions to improve living conditions, the Second Industrial Revolution proved a positive and beneficial time in American history. Each new invention snowballed, inspiring people on to a new age of discoveries and creativity. Lifestyles forever changed, with Americans moving from farms to cities to find work.

Most remarkable, starting with the Second Industrial Revolution, America continues to change the country and the world with amazing inventions. The United States has also pioneered the Third and Fourth Industrial Revolutions, introducing hitherto unimaginable discoveries and innovations, resulting in productivity surpassing expectations for each generation. "And in the end, it's not the years in your life that count. It's the life in your years," noted Abraham Lincoln, an American visionary leader and abolitionist who gave his life advocating equal rights for all.

Notes

1. Ryan Engelman, "The Second Industrial Revolution," *U.S. History Scene*, April 10, 2015, http://ushistoryscene.com/article/second-industrial-revolution/.
2. http://education.seattlepi.com/extent-did-industrial-revolution-change-american-social-economic-political-life-6960.html.
3. https://industrialdevelopement.weebly.com.
4. Ibid.
5. https://industrialdevelopement.weebly.com/working-conditions.html.
6. https://study.com/academy/lesson/labor-conditions-during-the-industrial-revolution-in-america.html.
7. https://industrialdevelopement.weebly.com/working-conditions.html.
8. https://courses.lumenlearning.com/boundless-ushistory/chapter/the-second-industrial-revolution/.
9. Ibid.
10. http://www.digitalhistory.uh.edu/disp_textbook.cfm?smtid=2&psid=3191.
11. Ibid.
12. Ibid.
13. http://www.history.com/topics/haymarket-riot.
14. http://www.digitalhistory.uh.edu/disp_textbook.cfm?smtid=2&psid=3191.
15. Ibid.
16. https://en.wikipedia.org/wiki/Fred_Harvey_(entrepreneur).
17. https://en.wikipedia.org/wiki/Atchison,_Topeka_and_Santa_Fe_Railway.
18. https://en.wikipedia.org/wiki/Great_Railroad_Strike_of_1877.
19. http://tammayauthor.com/index.php/2015/07/14/past-blast-tuesday-women-during-the-19th-century-industrial-revolution/.
20. Ibid.
21. https://industrialdevelopement.weebly.com/how-it-affects-us-today.html.
22. Ibid.
23. http://www.history.com/topics/womens-history/women-who-fought-for-the-vote.
24. Judith E. Harper, PBS.org, n.d., http://www.pbs.org/stantonanthony/resources/index.html?body=biography.html.
25. http://www.history.com/topics/womens-history/susan-b-anthony.
26. https://en.wikipedia.org/wiki/Victoria_Woodhull.
27. http://www.digitalhistory.uh.edu/disp_textbook.cfm?smtid=2&psid=3165.
28. Ibid.
29. Ibid.
30. Ibid.
31. Ibid.
32. http://www.digitalhistory.uh.edu/disp_textbook.cfm?smtid=2&psid=3167.
33. http://www.digitalhistory.uh.edu/disp_textbook.cfm?smtid=2&psid=3166.
34. http://www.ohiohistorycentral.org/w/Standard_Oil_Company.
35. http://www.digitalhistory.uh.edu/disp_textbook.cfm?smtid=2&psid=3166.
36. Ibid.

37. Ibid.
38. Ibid.
39. Ibid.
40. http://www.digitalhistory.uh.edu/disp_textbook.cfm?smtid=2&psid=3168.
41. https://en.wikipedia.org/wiki/Munn_v._Illinois.
42. Ibid.
43. Ibid.
44. http://www.digitalhistory.uh.edu/disp_textbook.cfm?smtid=2&psid=3169.
45. Ibid.
46. Ibid.
47. Ibid.
48. Ibid.
49. http://richmondvale.org/second-industrial-revolution/.

· 3 ·

THE THIRD INDUSTRIAL REVOLUTION

Introduction

The Third Industrial Revolution began in the 1970s, dramatically changing the world with the accelerated creation of digital technologies, in switching from mechanical and analog electrical technologies. Since it was affordable for almost everyone to acquire digital devices, this major world industrial revolution developed within a short timeframe—irrevocably changing our lifestyles forever. The Third Industrial Revolution was a key milestone marker in the history of humankind globally; it put technology into our hands, helping us become more productive, connected, and creating different lives to reflect our own unique career goals and aspirations.

Computers moved from being prohibitively expensive stationary and clumsy mainframes to desktops and lightweight laptops to mobile handheld smartphones. The World Wide Web and Internet opened up global frontiers 24/7, enabling people to communicate and trade nonstop, regardless of time zones. The human dimension connected people personally and professionally via Internet telecommunications (IT). Social media platforms for every imaginable lifestyle choice popped up from Facebook and Instagram, to professional connections such as LinkedIn.

Today, we rely on these digital technologies and platforms that continue to increase and change quickly, offering infinite *varieties* of content. Inescapably and inevitably, these quantum leaps have led to very different economies compared to the unwired lifestyles of the 1950s and 1960s. Also dubbed the Technology Revolution, Information Age, Computer Age, even New Media Age, the Third Industrial Revolution underpinned significant technological breakthroughs that took off, dynamically changing the world in ways unimaginable.

This period was significant as it paved the way for the Fourth Industrial Revolution. Big data analytics, artificial intelligence (AI) with machine and deep learning algorithms, robotics and automations, Internet of Things, and 3D printing are now ubiquitous in analyzing and supporting our digital-based consumer lifestyles.

Can you imagine life without your smartphone or laptop? In the short span of 30-plus years, two major industrial revolutions have significantly improved people's lives around the world. However, these earthshaking paradigm shifts are double-edged as well, tinged with darker shades of notoriety, spinning off on cybercrime with online hacking misappropriating funds and, worse, identity fraud.

For perspective, the First Industrial Revolution started in England in 1784, with mechanical production and steam-powered energy. From 1870, the Second Industrial Revolution boosted mass manufacturing with electrical energy. Another hundred years later, the Third Industrial Revolution burst forth in the 1970s with innovative digital technological applications.[1]

Software firms hyping huge investor returns were generously funded overnight; hiring increased exponentially with many companies offering BMWs as sign-on bonuses, stratospheric salaries were the norm, and excessive lifestyles of affluenza all spiraled out of control. But, prematurely grandiose returns on extreme and exuberant investments anticipated by investors giddy in getting rich quickly bombed. With the New Millennium, the "dot-com bubble" burst in 2000. (In hindsight, speculators caution about being overly optimistic in thinking "this time will be different.")

Overnight, the dot-com bomb littered the tech industry's landscape with company crashes and pervasive layoffs—with jobs harder to find in this sector. Expectations about salaries and job requirements muddied clarity about market worth. The Third Industrial Revolution changed the landscape moving forward, in terms of jobs and careers. More on the dot-com bubble in the last section of this chapter.

There are three important career lessons we learn from the Third Industrial Revolution dot-com boom and bust. First, employment is fickle, as people saw how they could be making lots of money one day—only to become unemployable the next. Second, layoffs are the norm in today's workplaces in shifting with changing technologies and consumer demands. Third, it forever nixed the concept of employees serving just one employer for life, and for those hankering for entrepreneurial success to learn the basics of business planning. (Many dot-com crashers did not have basic business plans to guide their business operations.)

The Third Industrial Revolution signaled the need for employers and employees alike to avoid career confusion. We all must learn to become adaptable and nimble in going with the flow of rapid-fire business changes affecting employment outcomes. You must acquire the mindset to be proactive to learn new career skill sets.

Whether layoffs are unexpected or expected, be mentally and emotionally strong—key being resilient in overcoming the odds. Armor yourself with the emotional and spiritual ability to pick up resolutely, stand tall, exhaust every possible career option, and become mentally prepared to seize opportunities for gainful employment again.

Trailblazing Technology Leaders of the Third Industrial Revolution

There are numerous groundbreaking tech visionaries who amazingly changed the world during the Third Industrial Revolution. Apple cofounders Steve Jobs and Steve Wozniak, Microsoft founder Bill Gates, HP founders Bill Hewlett and Dave Packard, database Oracle founder Larry Ellison, and legions more are the stuff of immortal legends. These tech leaders created devices, software, and computing services that we take for granted today in our daily activities (at workplace, in school, and businesses from one-person shops to mega corporations). Astoundingly, the fast pace of change picked up nonstop, with minimal disruptions. Ongoing tech innovations and enhancements were incessantly introduced, tempting consumers into buying upgrades for newer devices and ever more user-friendly software. Here are brief summaries of tech companies that have impacted, and continue to impact, our lives with digital technologies.

Xerox Corporation

Xerox's (xerox.com) digital footprint is indelibly imprinted around the world with the pivotal role it plays in print history, in constantly imagining forward-thinking digital imaging. In creating photocopying machines for homes and businesses with digital computing, Xerox printers morphed into a worldwide presence to "xerox" or photocopy paper documents—forever fostering its name into a memorable meme. Since 2008, to xerox has become part of our everyday vernacular. Taking huge steps (including risky ideas) to keep on creating continues with Xerox's slogan: "The best way to predict the future is to invent it."

In 1970, Xerox founded the influential Palo Alto Research Center (PARC, parc.com). Instead of sequestering PARC within Xerox, the company's vision calls for collaboration to innovate products, to research and refine upon business processes that are nimble, and to enable sustainable enterprises to keep inventing useful digital products. This forward-thinking vision builds on cofounders Joseph C. Wilson and Chester Carlson, formerly the Haloid Photographic Company. Founded on April 18, 1906, Xerox has a venerable history.

Xerox introduced two important elements facilitating desktop personal computing. PARC engineers invented the graphical user interface (GUI) in 1970 based on a desktop metaphor, with menus and task bars for organizing folders and files. The first commercial mouse debuted in 1973 with the Xerox Alto, an early personal computer (PC). However, the board of directors at Xerox shifted focus and allowed their engineers to share PC concepts with Apple technicians for three days in exchange for 100,000 Apple shares. Later, Microsoft also adopted these desktop configurations for personal computing— and the rest is history.[2] Xerox with its pixilated "X" icon maintains a global edge with innovative user applications and is a socially responsible contributor for sustainable digital technologies into the Third and Fourth Industrial Revolutions.

IBM

International Business Machines (or IBM; ibm.com), aka "Big Blue," was started by Thomas J. Watson, Jr. in 1924. Watson reconfigured an existing recordkeeping company to provide automated business support services. IBM soon became synonymous with electric typewriters. In the 1960s, IBM continued providing business services to government agencies and large corporations with massive mainframe computer hardware and customized software. However, in focusing on these services to mega businesses, IBM lost out to the lucrative PC revolution targeting individuals (thus enabling Microsoft to gain ground and dominance).

IBM has retooled and rebounded.[3] In 2017, IBM continued its historic 25-year run as the leading holder of U.S. patents (topping Samsung and Intel), reported *Investor's Business Daily*.[4] In 2012, Virginia Marie "Ginni" Rometty who started as an IBM engineer in 1981 became its first woman chairperson, president, and CEO. *Forbes* business magazine noted that under Rometty's leadership, IBM turned around a 21-year decline by focusing on providing data services such as "cognitive computing" (more commonly called artificial intelligence or AI) and cloud computing services.[5]

IBM's strategic move to provide businesses with digital support services capitalized on resurrecting AI, incorporating algorithms for machine learning. IBM has succeeded in positioning its Watson brand as the leading AI brand in the industry. Named after the founder, this switch also fittingly acknowledged the contributions of IBM engineer Arthur Samuel, who had coined the term *machine learning* back in 1959. Samuel developed a software program to play checkers, with the capability to learn from its machine-playing experiences.[6]

I graduated a math major in the 1960s, and lived in New York. IBM recruited math majors to move to San Francisco to work on new technology projects. We were a small group of women math majors. IBM offered to train us. I went and lived in Haight Ashbury, a very wild time to be in San Francisco. I stayed out west, in technology. It was very exciting.

—Project Manager, Information Technology

Apple, Inc.

Steve Jobs is forever associated with founding Apple, Inc. (apple.com) on April 1, 1976. Less well known are cofounders Steve "Woz" Wozniak and Ronald Wayne. However, Wayne left three weeks later and the two Steves incorporated their company on January 3, 1977. Jobs and Woz were high-school friends who dropped out and went to work for Silicon Valley companies—Jobs at Atari, "Woz" at Hewlett-Packard (HP). Woz was the whiz who designed and hand-built Apple I. Jobs masterminded sales for Apple I, at $666.66 per machine.[7]

On January 24, 1984 Apple introduced the first Macintosh PC, or Mac, promising to change the world with PC technology. However, in losing a power tussle with his mentor and then Apple CEO John Sculley, Steve Jobs left in May 1985—relinquishing his leadership of Apple's Macintosh division. Yet, this sushi- and soba-loving Zen Buddhist who was neither engineer, programmer, nor MBA never settled for less. Jobs instinctively adopted a spiritual approach incorporating beauty, design functionality, and user-friendly components for Apple products upon returning to Apple in February 1997.

A business genius, Jobs created "Genius Bars" in Apple stores to educate and entice customers. Apple's first two retail stores opened on May 19, 2001 at Tysons Corner Center in MacLean, Virginia, and in Glendale, California. Since then, over 500 Apple stores have opened around the world. Thanks to Apple's digital devices with the iPod streaming music (introduced October 23, 2001), iPhone (released June 29, 2007), and iPad tablet (launched January 27, 2010), plus other innovative products and services, Apple is on its way to top a market capitalization of a trillion dollars by 2019.[8]

> I sent a cold call email to Steve Jobs pitching my recruiting services with no expectation that he would read it. I received a phone call from his Chief of Staff five minutes later saying Steve was impressed because I went to the top of the organization to get his business. He signed the contract that day and I got the executive search for his VP of Sales.
>
> —Recruiting firm, President

Microsoft

Microsoft cofounders Bill Gates and Paul Allen (then aged 19 and 22, respectively) started the company on April 4, 1975 in Albuquerque, New Mexico. Because it was a challenge to recruit top programmers in "Querque," Microsoft relocated to Redmond, Washington (Gates and Allen's home state) on January 1, 1979. The duo partnered with IBM in 1980 to bundle operating support (OS/1, then OS/2) for IBM machines and were paid a royalty for each sale.

Meanwhile, Gates and Allen cloned and sold their own PC machines, calling their operating support Windows. With each new iteration of Windows, Microsoft's operating support continued to outperform IBM's OS/2. By the 1990s, Microsoft outclassed behemoth Big Blue to capture 90 percent of the world's PC market.[9]

Digital computing continues to define Microsoft's leading edge in the Third Industrial Revolution under third CEO, Satya Nadella from India who took over on February 4, 2014. Like IBM, Microsoft advances strategically at this writing by focusing on AI. At the heart of AI is the smart mining of messy data generated by billions of disparate online users from around the globe. Every e-mail post, photo-sharing, website use, and online activity is mined by mathematical algorithms, harnessing machine and deep learning processes that continuously sift through and refine upon user data. Little wonder that in 2016 Microsoft paid $26.2 billion for LinkedIn, the business social media platform for professionals. In August 2017, Microsoft's real-time AI applications for its Azure cloud enterprise customers enhanced real-time consumer pricing and customer personalization.[10]

Hewlett and Packard (HP)

Stanford University located in Palo Alto, California, just south of San Francisco is synonymous with Silicon Valley's birthplace at 367 Addison Avenue—the garage where engineering students William R. Hewlett and David Packard began building HP products (hpe.com) starting January 1, 1939. The duo's first HP product was an audio oscillator (HP200A), customized for Walt Disney Studios to amplify Disney's first stereophonic sound movie, *Fantasia*.[11]

Serendipitously situated in advancing Silicon Valley as the Third Industrial Revolution's global center for advanced digital technology, HP's garage is only a 15-minute drive to Jobs and Woz' Apple garage at 2066 Crist Avenue in Los Altos.[12] As cosmic was then 12-year-old Steve Jobs' first cold call to Bill Hewlett for advice on a school project. Later, between freshman and sophomore high school years, Jobs worked for HP at this HP garage.[13]

Today, HP continues the tradition of creating customized technological innovations for business transformation. For instance, Hewlett Packard Labs develop leading-edge technology for computing power (estimated at 100 billion devices by 2020), memory-driven computing to cure Alzheimer's (symptoms develop 20 years prior, and scientists hope to catch prognoses earlier), and blockchain software underpinning cryptocurrencies such as Bitcoin.[14]

Cisco Systems, Inc.

Cisco Systems (cisco.com) is the world's largest networking company developing and manufacturing IT systems. Founders Leonard Bosack and Sandy

Lerner, Stanford computer scientists who started Cisco in December 1984, pioneered the local area network (LAN) system connecting computers from various places using a multiple-channel router system. Bosack managed computers at Stanford's computer science department, while his wife Sandy managed Stanford's Graduate School of Business computers. The name "Cisco" is a derivative of San Francisco, as Silicon Valley is just south of the Bay Area.[15]

John Morgridge (Cisco CEO, 1988–1995) was frugal. I was assigned as his corporate escort at the Nobel Peace Prize ceremony in Norway. My role was to make sure he made it to the event on time and meet key customers. Security called me in a panic. John did not take the special limo to bring him to the hotel. Everyone was distraught. In true form, John decided to take the train and walk to the hotel in the snow. He did not want to waste money on a limo.

—Tracey Wilen

Incredibly, when the dot-com bubble burst in 2000, Cisco was the most highly valued company on the planet with a market capitalization of $500 billion. While this valuation has dropped significantly owing to the shift from LAN systems to internet protocols seamlessly combining both routing and switching, Cisco continues to create computer hardware products while also offering cloud computing services, plus expanding globally.

I had a flat tax opinion paper due for my economics class. I was at a Cisco dinner with John Chambers (Cisco CEO, 1995–2015). He was concerned I was leaving early. I explained the situation. He said, "I have a lot of opinions (pro) about flat tax. You interview me at dinner and then your assignment will be done and you can stay." I did interview him and submitted the paper. It was graded a "C" paper because the professor did not believe I interviewed John Chambers and she also did not agree with John's point of view.

—Tracey Wilen

Oracle Corporation

Meanwhile, Oracle (oracle.com) developed database management software for all that information and content churned out nonstop by individuals, households, businesses, and research centers. Founded in 1977 by Larry Ellison, Bob Miner, and Ed Oates, Oracle also develops software for enterprise resource planning, supply chain management, and customer service management.

Oracle Cloud's computing services offer servers, storage, networking, and other applications through managed data centers around the world.

On January 27, 2010, Oracle acquired Sun Microsystems (then valued at over $7 billion) and began manufacturing hardware, too. Oracle's expansion kept gobbling up various acquisitions around the world, leading to its development of global business units serving industries in communications, construction and engineering, finance, health care, hospitality, retail, and utilities.[16]

I met Scott Mc Nealy (Sun Microsystems CEO, 1984–2006) at Meg Whitman's (HP CEO, 2001–2017) garden party. He is a pragmatic business guy known to say, "Technology has the shelf life of a banana." He discussed his new role as the CEO of Wayin, a social marketing firm. He invited me to visit the launch at the Consumer Electronics Show (CES) show. I did and it was very exciting to see the next evolution of technology.
—Tracey Wilen

Intel Corporation

Intel (intel.com) builds microchip processors, the vital silicon chip for computers to run on. Founded July 18, 1968 by Gordon Moore and Robert Noyce, Intel sells processors to computer makers such as Apple, Dell, HP, and Lenovo. Noyce, a physicist, was a leading inventor of the microchip (aka integrated circuit or CPU, computer processing unit). Moore, a chemist, lent his name to Moore's Law, which accurately predicted the number of transistors in a microchip doubling every two years—helpful for target planning research and development projects.

Working for Andy Grove (Intel CEO, 1979–1998) was difficult. He was confrontational and abrupt. We would scatter if he walked into the company cafeteria as he would approach people and ask, "What did you do today to increase Intel's stock?"
—Intel Marketing Manager

Intel produced the world's first commercial microchip processor in 1971, but it wasn't until 20 years later that it focused on producing microchip processors for PCs—in conjunction with Microsoft, Apple, and other PC makers' meteoric sales. Since 1992, Intel has maintained its dominance as the world's top microchip maker. However, smartphones and tablet computers today primarily use processors from ARM, a British firm; amidst declining PC sales, this is a challenge for Intel to retool and repurpose its vision.[17]

Motorola

Motorola (motorola.com) founded on September 25, 1928 by the Galvin brothers, Paul V. and Joseph E., in Chicago produced battery-powered radios using electricity in the home plus car radio receivers to law enforcement agencies in Illinois. Motorola incorporated it in 1947 and specialized in manufacturing TV sets and radios. In 1960, Motorola produced the world's first transistorized, cordless 19-inch portable TV. Astronaut Neil Armstrong, the first man on the moon in 1969, spoke his immortal line, "One small step for a man, one giant leap for mankind," into a Motorola transceiver.

Forward wind to 1973; Motorola produced the first handheld portable phone. In 1974 the company made its first microprocessor and went on to pioneer a new generation 32-bit microprocessor in 1980 that was vital for building PCs. Apple, Atari, and HP were many companies that used Motorola's 32-bit CPU.

By 1998, two-thirds of the company's gross revenues came from cell phones. However, in 2010, Motorola sold its cellular infrastructure division to Finland's Nokia Siemens Network.[18]

World Wide Web

The Third Industrial Revolution was epochal, heralding accessibility and affordability for people to find information on the World Wide Web (www) powered by digital technology. Web browsers further made it easy to type in words and phrases to surf the Web for specialized information, freely and conveniently at any hour of day or night, regardless of time zones. Billions of people could almost overnight communicate, interact, and conduct lucrative businesses across space and time—by selling products and services to consumers with search engine optimized websites. In time, companies such as Amazon morphed into Internet behemoths with online e-commerce.

English scientist Tim Berners-Lee invented the World Wide Web in 1989 while working at CERN, the European organization for nuclear research, in Switzerland. Berners-Lee's web browser software was released to government and research institutions in January 1991; by August 1991, it was released to the public. Fittingly, the first server outside of Europe was installed at Stanford Linear Accelerator Center in December 1991.

In 1993, a graphical web browser called Mosaic, launched by the National Center for Supercomputing Applications at the University of Illinois at Urbana-Champaign, provided a critical turning point in facilitating Web applications. Mosaic's user interface incorporated text and graphics.

While often used in the same breath, the World Wide Web is distinct from the Internet. The Internet is a worldwide computer network space; the World Wide Web consists of digital documents linked by hyperlinks and identified by uniform resource locators (URLs). Websites are created by, and for, global browsers and users—thanks to ever-increasing user-friendly and affordable digital enhancements dished up by the Third Industrial Revolution.[19]

The Internet initially began as the Pentagon's ARPANET project, with funding provided by the U.S. government, which had envisioned a World Wide Web as early as the 1940s to connect researchers. Vint Cerf (currently with Google), a cocreator of the Internet, attributes the Internet's early successes to Xerox's Ethernet protocol, the Xerox Alto PC, Xerox Network System, and PARC Universal packet. Detailed design started at Stanford in 1974, followed by worldwide implementation in 1975 at Stanford, University College London, and other research venues. However, in reality, collaborative efforts of scientists around the world helped create the Internet.[20]

Google LLC

Google search engine founders, Sergey Brin and Larry Page, another pair of whizzes with a Stanford pedigree, were PhD students. While Google began in January 1996 as a research project running as google.standford.edu, the founders formally incorporated on September 4, 1998. An early Google angel investor grasped the significance of Google's vision—Amazon founder, Jeff Bezos. Brin and Page rented a garage in Silicon Valley at 232 Santa Margarita Avenue in Menlo Park, a few miles from Apple's iconic garage.[21]

Now located at Googleplex in Mountain View, California, Google's meteoric ascent saw it reorganizing multifarious acquisitions and ensuing operations in August 2015. Alphabet, Inc. became the parent conglomerate with Larry Page as CEO. Google the search engine and related Internet activities continues as Alphabet's primary subsidiary under another Indian-born CEO, Sundar Pichai.

> While a Stanford visiting scholar, our small group met alumni and professors who were changing the world with technology inventions. We were invited to meet Sergey Brin a PhD student who co-created Google. I remember he was wearing "Vibram five-finger shoes." He explained in very simple terms the potential of search. It was a very exciting session and we all knew it was going to be big. We of course all asked him if we could work there, but he said it was early days and perhaps in the future.
>
> —Tracey Wilen

Google, another American conglomerate at the forefront of digital revolutions spawned by Silicon Valley in the Third Industrial Revolution, continues to grow exponentially. The most visited website is Google.com. Google purchased YouTube in 2006 for $1.65 billion, furthering its lead in digital tech with video browsing benefiting Google, while monetizing YouTubers.[22]

In addition to Google's top-ranked Chrome cloud-based web browser, its vision includes holding the lead in mobile digital technology with Android, the free operating support for smartphones. In May 2017, Gartner, Inc. reported Android dominated global smartphone operating support at 86.1 percent market share, and Apple's iOS at 13.7 percent. Silicon Valley's Google and Apple control almost 100 percent of all global smartphone operating support.[23]

Amazon.com, Inc.

Amazon (amazon.com) is ubiquitous with online retailing and retail industry's indisputable leader. Founded by Jeff Bezos on July 5, 1994 as Cadabra, Inc., it changed the name to Amazon a year later. This e-retailer initially sold books, then streamed audio books and music—plus rapidly expanding into innumerable diverse categories including fashion and food.[24]

Forever deep-mining the frontiers of e-commerce with digital technologies and consumer data using computer learning and AI algorithms, Amazon opened brick-mortar bookstores; the first one on November 2, 2015 in Seattle's University Village.[25] On January 22, 2018, the world's first digi-powered convenience store, Amazon Go, premiered in downtown Seattle. The free Amazon Go app is pegged to Apple's iOS and Google's Android. With just a swish of your smartphone upon entering a turnstile, you put away your phone, shop, and check out without having to wait in line.[26] (We discuss the Fourth

Industrial Revolution's impact on AI and deep learning, including privacy concerns, in the next chapter.)

With over half a million employees worldwide, this e-commerce giant extended its digital impact with Amazon Web Services (AWS), a cloud-based enterprise. Massive not only in terms of employees, Amazon has rapidly ascended as the world's fourth most valuable publicly traded company as of December 31, 2017 after Apple, Inc., Alphabet, Inc., and Microsoft (based on the *Financial Times*' "Global 500" rankings). Since 2015, Amazon has surpassed Walmart as America's largest retailer.[27]

PayPal Holdings, Inc.

With the sheer volume, variety, and velocity of business dealings trading goods and services nonstop 24/7, it was clear digital payments systems were due. PayPal (paypal.com) first stepped up to the plate in December 1999. PayPal is active in over 200 countries.[28]

Facebook

Facebook (fb.com), the foremost social media platform for social networking, began on February 4, 2004, created by Harvard sophomore Mark Zuckerberg who dropped out to follow his passion. (Harvard dropout Microsoft cofounder Bill Gates was Zuckerberg's most-admired hero.) A swift four months later, Facebook moved to Menlo Park in Silicon Valley. That same month, PayPal cofounder Peter Thiel became Facebook's first investor. Since then, Facebook reportedly has over 2 billion users, hugely profiting from advertising revenues.[29]

Takeaways

The major takeaway from these mega American tech companies and their worldwide impact in the Third Industrial Revolution is—it pays to start small, in humble garages or dorm rooms, and then harness the boundless potential of digital technology with perspicacity and ingenuity, to grow into global giants. Digital technologies are here to stay, forever changing people's lives in myriad ways, however unfathomable for the moment.

Given such a powerful foothold into every sector of society by companies like Amazon, Apple, and Google, new avenues for career choices are constantly opening up. What steps are you taking to empower your career aspirations to playing big, in your own unique way?

Another observation is how visionaries astutely discern digital technologies for their far-reaching benefits. For instance, Amazon founder Jeff Bezos was an angel investor in Google; PayPal cofounder Peter Thiel was Facebook's first investor. How would you prepare to recognize career opportunities as they open up, or become inspired to start your own business?

However, not all is glitz and glam. Similar to previous gold rushes, digital fortune hunters experienced ups-and-downs with the industry's dot-com boom and bust. I worked for Apple and Cisco. I share an experience in the section below.

Tech Employment during the Third Industrial Revolution

Dot-com Boom 1990–2000

During the 1990–2000 dot-com boom or tech bubble, Silicon Valley was in its heyday of living large, when overinvesting went amuck for any kind of computer-related start-up. With the high demand for workers, hiring went out of control, reflected in stratospheric salaries and outsized signing-on bonuses. During this brief tech boom, national U.S. employment rate in this sector increased by 36 percent, with average wages doubling. Yet tech employment was only 4 percent of all private jobs.

These figures are from the Federal Reserve Bank of St. Louis. When the tech bubble burst in 2000, the number of techies employed fell from 17.8 percent to 3.4 percent in 2004. Tech employment offers higher than average wages, but these jobs come with caveats. Tech industry jobs have historically shifted between boom-and-bust, expansion and contraction.[30] Such employment gyrations of course produce confounding career choices and emotional consequences for people unaccustomed to rapid hiring and firing.

According to the Federal Reserve Bank of St. Louis, a techie earned $1.60 for every dollar that a private-sector employee earned, in 1990. In 2015, it increased to $2.20 for the average techie. Up to 1996, about 60 percent of tech jobs were in manufacturing—compared to 80 percent of tech workers in professional services by 2015.[31]

"I kind of miss the days of obscene compensation."

Figure 3.1. Source: ©Cartoon Resource.

Nevertheless, Silicon Valley remains an innovative hub fueling the Third and Fourth Industrial Revolutions. The U.S. Bureau of Labor Statistics examined the area's employment data from 2001 to 2008; it found ongoing high wages in the tech sector continues Silicon Valley's ability to evolve, to reinvent itself with ingenuity, and in forging ahead with technological advancement.[32]

Living the Dot-com Bubble

With oodles of money to burn (and no business plans to plug profits) dot-com startup CEOs lived outrageously and extravagantly. For example, Ernst Malmsten, founder of e-fashion retailer Boo.com, blew $135 million of venture capital in 18 months. His enduring quote was, "After the pampered luxury of a Lear Jet 35, Concorde was a bit cramped." Famed for its sock-puppet ads, Pet.com founder Greg LeMore raised $121 million in August 1998, but folded 268 days later. After founding Borders Bookstores in 1971, Louis Borders started the online grocery venture WebVan in 1999—and went bankrupt in two years.[33]

"Guess what just happened to our stock price?!"

Figure 3.2. Source: ©Cartoon Resource.

Obviously, people learn from making mistakes, but outsized living without accountable results played its part, too. Many tech startups had no business plans, and got off by hyping their Internet cache. Wall Street investors were giddy with the thought of getting rich overnight with tech stocks—and failed to understand the lack of valuation each tech company overhyped.

When the Tech Bubble Burst

When did the tech bubble burst, and why? In the early 1990s, there were few Internet companies—and they were truly top-tier quality firms. By the mid-1990s as these early Internet firms began showing their growth worth, all of a sudden investors became enamored with tech stocks. Two years, 1996–1998, were especially noteworthy when demand from venture capitalists to invest outstripped the supply of Internet companies worthy of their investments.

In 1999 with money-losing ventures tanking, Wall Street swooned in the opposite direction: Internet stocks lost $1.7 trillion. However, early 1990s investors were spared since they had invested in the real deals. The Bloomberg Internet Index of 280 stocks fell to $1.193 trillion from their peak of $2.948, with the $1.7 trillion hemorrhage occurring in just six months, between March and September, 2000. Only five of these 280 stocks were down less than 5 percent.[34]

Just as suddenly, job losses and layoffs spun out of control, too. Techies and non-techies employed by Internet firms got laid off overnight. Unprepared to being let go off so unexpectedly, people were forced to unlearn and retool their employable skills for other employment opportunities. Thousands were stunned directionless and forced to seek counseling.

Unemployed techies turned up at "Pink Slip Parties" commiserating with each other and networking to find their next jobs. While partygoers had not officially been served individual pink slips from being let off by firms that crashed, there were $2 pink drinks (pink martini or pint of beer), free food, and free admission at Pink Slip Parties. In reality though, tech companies sponsored these parties, scouting for top techies whom they hoped would fit into their company cultures—quite different from spontaneous pink-slip parties when dot-coms crashed and good-byes were unceremoniously held that same night at local bars.[35] Pink Slip Parties generated press from as far away as London, as reported by the Guardian.[36]

**"I had a golden parachute, but lost it in a downsizing.
This one's made of corrugated cardboard."**

Figure 3.3. Source: ©Cartoon Resource.

Yet, as in every industry, top talent who consistently give their best can survive a dot-com, or any industry, crash. Point being, top talent is rarer. In the Third and Fourth Industrial Revolutions, new jobs are constantly created faster than new recruits can come up to speed, so top talent will prevail in moving on to the next gig.[37] It pays to stay on top of your career aspirations (instead of being shell-shocked by pink slips through no fault of your own) and to be determined in doing due diligence to stay ahead.

The Dot-bomb was memorable, but the Great Recession (2007–2009) was devastating. I (as a recruiter) started the Palo Alto Wine Meetup group in 2007 to help people find jobs. I invited people to my home for a glass of wine and offered to critique resumes and give job hunting tips. The group grew to over 5,000 members at its peak, so we met in restaurants around Palo Alto, California. Today many of the people I helped are employed, stay in touch with me and now give job openings to my firm. It feels good to help people when they need it most.

—Recruiting firm President

Women in the Digital Workforce

During this era, the American Federation of State, County and Municipal Employees reported women enjoyed the highest participation in national leadership positions.[38] Women are gaining more leadership advancement ground in the tech industry, too. *Fortune* magazine's annual "*Fortune* 500" rankings of top companies noted in June 2017, "the four highest-paid female CEOs ... all run tech companies." Listed in order, they are: (1) Safra Catz, Oracle co-CEO; (2) Meg Whitman, HP Enterprise CEO, (3) Ginni Rometty, IBM CEO, and (4) Marissa Mayer, former Yahoo CEO.[39]

I am very lucky to live in Silicon Valley. I have met many successful women in business and technology. I had the pleasure of meeting Meg Whitman, Sheryl Sandberg, Marissa Meyers, and Indra Nooyi, to name a few. I think it is important for women to have female role models. I encourage women to attend conferences with female keynote speakers and watch talks by women in their industries to learn how to achieve success in their roles.
—Tracey Wilen

This online *Fortune* article points out all four women have a STEM (Science, Technology, Engineering, and Math) background. Moreover, professional fields with the highest returns are computer science and engineering (electrical, mechanical, and chemical industrial). However, more discouraging is the trend that fewer women today are entering STEM fields compared to the 1980s.

Separate from the tech industry's highest paid female CEOs listed earlier is *Fortune*'s October 2017 (20th edition) ranking of "The 50 Most Powerful Women" who are not necessarily CEOs. *Fortune* recognized nine tech female leaders in this order:

Sheryl Sandberg, Facebook COO, fifth
Ginni Rometty, IBM CEO, sixth
Meg Whitman, HP Enterprise CEO, seventh
Safra Catz, Oracle co-CEO, eighth
Ruth Porat, Alphabet Inc., SVP and CFO, tenth
Angela Ahrendts, Apple SVP, Retail, thirteenth
Susan Wojcicki, YouTube CEO (now part of Google), fourteenth
Amy Hood, Microsoft EVP & CFO, twenty-sixth
Bridget van Kralingen, IBM SVP, Industry Platforms, fortieth
Nine of the powerful fifty women recognized by *Fortune* in 2017 are in the tech industry—an amazing achievement in a forward-moving arena where women can shine.[40]

Tracey's Transition Tips

People worked hard, and all the time, at Apple. After a year, I noticed that despite great reviews, I wasn't promoted and couldn't understand why. The men who came after me were given more opportunities and management positions. I was told I wouldn't get ahead unless I had a master's in engineering or business, and that I was not technical enough. I proposed Apple enroll me into San Jose State University's MBA/Apple Partnership reserved for managers and take technology classes typically reserved for engineers. They agreed.

- You are a revenue stream. If you perceive barriers to your income potential, understand why and find a solution(s).
- Overcome job obstacles by addressing concerns head on, in positive ways.
- Engage in constant communication with your manager and provide win–win solutions.
- Take advantage of educational packages your firm offers while there. You will expand your skills and become more valuable.

Summary

The Third Industrial Revolution has forever changed career paths moving forward, for the need to shift with new technology meeting consumer demands. In addition to voluminous online content generated, the sheer *variety*, and *velocity* at which information is exchanged (including the need to *verify* content), and the *volatility* of job creation, the need for individuals to adapt to unexpected career changes is paramount.

It is important to point out that growing firms show increasing job creation, whereas large firms hire at a slower pace due to size and organizational layers of bureaucracy. Innovative startups with strong business plans driven by top talent will thrive, in moving forward with a strong vision to collaborate—while highlighting their unique core competencies.

- Technology is here to stay, to change lives, firms, industries, education, and careers.
- Employment is fickle. People saw how they could be making a lot of money one day and then become unemployable the next.
- Layoffs have become a natural part of people's lives; the concept of one employer for life has transitioned away.
- Technology has a large foothold in firms and industries, in driving the economy forward. Amazon, Google, and Apple are large firms hiring in many diverse sectors.

- Individuals, employers, and policy-makers must be aware of how the employment landscape changes constantly—and proactive in keeping up with industry trends and needs.

Notes

1. Hamish McRae, "Davos 2016: Forget the markets—the Fourth Industrial Revolution is here," *The Independent*, January 23, 2016, http://www.independent.co.uk/voices/davos-2016-forget-the-markets-the-fourth-industrial-revolution-is-here-a6830491.html. UBS Global Topics. Davos 2016. White Paper on the Fourth Industrial Revolution, https://www.ubs.com/global/en/about_ubs/follow_ubs/highlights/davos-2016.html. Klaus Schwab, "The Fourth Industrial Revolution: what it means, how to respond," World Economic Forum, https://www.weforum.org/agenda/2016/01/the-fourth-industrial-revolution-what-it-means-and-how-to-respond/.
2. https://en.wikipedia.org/wiki/Xerox; https://en.wikipedia.org/wiki/Apple_Inc.
3. https://en.wikipedia.org/wiki/History_of_IBM.
4. *Investor's Business Daily*, https://www.nasdaq.com/article/ibm-holds-patent-lead-for-25th-straight-year-samsung-intel-follow-cm902685.
5. https://www.forbes.com/profile/ginni-rometty/.
6. Harry McCracken, "The Great AI War of 2018," *Fast Company*, November 2017, 64–73.
7. https://en.wikipedia.org/wiki/Apple_Inc.
8. George Beahm, *Steve Jobs' Life by Design* (New York: Palgrave Macmillan, 2014).
9. https://en.wikipedia.org/wiki/History_of_Microsoft.
10. Harry McCracken, "The Great AI War of 2018," *Fast Company*, November 2017, 73.
11. https://en.wikipedia.org/wiki/HP_Garage.
12. Damon Darlin, "Shrine to Hours of Tinkering in a Garage on the Ground Floor of Silicon Valley," *New York Times*, December 4, 2005, http://www.nytimes.com/2005/12/04/us/shrine-to-hours-of-tinkering-in-a-garage-on-the-ground-floor-of-silicon.html.
13. George Beahm, *Steve Jobs' Life by Design* (New York: Palgrave Macmillan, 2014), 16.
14. https://www.labs.hpe.com/.
15. https://en.wikipedia.org/wiki/Cisco_Systems.
16. https://en.wikipedia.org/wiki/Oracle_Corporation.
17. https://en.wikipedia.org/wiki/Intel.
18. https://en.wikipedia.org/wiki/Motorola.
19. https://en.wikipedia.org/wiki/World_Wide_Web.
20. Colin Wood, "Who Really, Really Invented the Internet?" July 27, 2012, *Government Technology*, http://www.govtech.com/e-government/Who-Invented-the-Internet.html.
21. Damon Darlin, "Shrine to Hours of Tinkering in a Garage on the Ground Floor of Silicon Valley," *New York Times*, December 4, 2005, http://www.nytimes.com/2005/12/04/us/shrine-to-hours-of-tinkering-in-a-garage-on-the-ground-floor-of-silicon.html.
22. https://en.wikipedia.org/wiki/Google.
23. https://www.gartner.com/newsroom/id/3725117.
24. https://en.wikipedia.org/wiki/Amazon_(company).

25. Lisa Eadicicco, "Look Inside Amazon's First Physical Store," *Time*, November 4, 2015. http://time.com/4099690/amazon-books-bookstore/.

26. https://www.amazon.com/b?ie=UTF8&node=16008589011.

27. https://en.wikipedia.org/wiki/List_of_public_corporations_by_market_capitalization#-Publicly_traded_companies.

28. https://en.wikipedia.org/wiki/PayPal.

29. https://en.wikipedia.org/wiki/Facebook.

30. Charles S. Gascon & Evan Karson, "Growth in Tech Sector Returns to Glory Days of the 1990s," *The Regional Economist*, Second Quarter, 2017, https://www.stlouisfed.org/publications/regional-economist/second-quarter-2017/growth-in-tech-sector-returns-to-glory-days-of-the-1990s.

31. Federal Reserve Bank of St. Louis, August 15, 2017, https://www.stlouisfed.org/on-the-economy/2017/august/tech-employment-returns-heights.

32. Amar Nann & Tony Nunes, "After the Dot-Com Bubble: Silicon Valley High-Tech Employment and Wages in 2001 and 2008," *Bureau of Statistics Regional Report*, August 2009. https://www.bls.gov/opub/regional_reports/200908_silicon_valley_high_tech.htm.

33. Jim Edwards, "One of the kings of the '90s dot-com bubble now faces 20 years in prison," *Business Insider*, December 6, 2016, http://www.businessinsider.com/where-are-the-kings-of-the-1990s-dot-com-bubble-bust-2016-12/#joseph-parks-kozmo-was-the-frothiest-disaster-of-the-first-dotcom-bubble-according-to-wired-and-it-burned-250-million-but-like-a-zombie-it-has-somehow-come-back-to-life-11.

34. David Kleinbard, "The $1.7 trillion dot.com lesson," *CNN Money*, November 9, 2000, http://money.cnn.com/2000/11/09/technology/overview/.

35. Sam Whiting, "Think Pink Slip/Layoff Parties to come to Silicon Valley," *SF Gate*, March 7, 2001, https://www.sfgate.com/bayarea/article/Think-Pink-Slip-Layoff-parties-to-come-to-2945029.php.

36. Duncan Campbell, "Pink slip parties cure dot.com blues in San Francisco," *Guardian*, January 28, 2001, https://www.theguardian.com/technology/2001/jan/29/internetnews.internationalnews.

37. Sacha Cohen, "Lessons from the dot-com layoffs", *IT World*, December 8, 2000, https://www.itworld.com/article/2783676/careers/lessons-from-the-dot-com-layoffs.html.

38. https://www.afscme.org/for-members/womens-leadership-training/leadership-tools/body/Women_in_Labor_History_Timeline.pdf.

39. Valentina Zarya, "Here's What the Highest-Paid Female CEOs Have in Common," *Fortune*, June 20, 2017, fortune.com/2017/06/20/female-fortune-500-ceo/.

40. Kristen Bellstrom & Beth Kowitt, "50 Most Powerful Women," *Fortune*, October 1, 2017, 54–66.

· 4 ·

THE FOURTH INDUSTRIAL REVOLUTION

Introduction

Currently, a significant portion of the annual gross domestic product (GDP)—between 8 and 16 percent—in developed countries is spent on astronomical healthcare expenditures (for medical tests and visits, hospitalizations, pharmaceutical costs, etc.). In the United States, this amount is larger than the amount spent on manufacturing. What if advanced medical apps capable of diagnosing symptoms before illnesses developed, were capable of transmitting data to specialist treatment centers? Where smart machines "talked" to each other, omitting doctor and specialist fees? The saving grace is for patients to consult a physician only as needed, not as a routine procedure, with people taking responsibility to maintain personal health and well-being. Healthcare costs would plummet tremendously, with patient outcomes vastly enhanced.[1]

Imagine if you needed a new knee, nose, ear, or kidney, you could place an order for a body part replacement customized to match your own cellular DNA specifications so your body wouldn't reject your new implant. Thanks to 3D printing, if indeed you needed a new ear, it is now possible to fabricate a 3D polymer mold to implant your ear mold with your own stem cells. Moreover, instead of an invasive bone marrow transplant, stem cells from your fat cells can grow healthy new cartilage, muscles, even new bone, with 3D bioprinting.[2]

Other forms of bioprinting include producing a healthy new liver, as scientists at the University of California San Diego discovered. Using a patient's stem cells from their skin that are cultivated in vitro for three weeks allows stem cells to grow into normal liver cells. Upon testing, these cells performed beautifully like a live liver—secreting albumin and producing urea and higher-level enzymes capable of metabolizing drugs. The payoff continues. It takes about 12 years and $1.8 billion of rounds of clinical trials and testing for one drug to gain FDA approval. However, with 3D printed tissue, pharmaceutical companies can begin testing sooner, and winnow down to faster testing timeframes using the most promising drugs.[3]

If your family had a history of genetic disorders, gene splicing is in order to correct issues prior to baby's birth. In experimenting with dozens of embryos, scientists successfully corrected a genetic heart defect in nearly two-thirds of embryos. Astoundingly, no potential mutations occurred in the embryos' DNA.[4]

Are you in a hurry for Amazon to drop off baby formula and diapers within 30 minutes? Rest assured "Amazon Prime Air" drone delivery service ably flies up to the plate, lands on your Amazon helipad mat flagged out on your yard, and drops off those essentials before flying on home. The mats are lightweight and roll away for storage. For now, drones strictly fly 15 miles roundtrip, max. If you're stuck out in the sticks away from an Amazon distribution center, you're out of luck. But not for long, surely, given Amazon's vision and tireless inventive genius.[5]

On a trans-Pacific flight, at mid-air and mid-way, your captain calmly radioed that your smart plane noticed an engine rotor needed fixing. Immediately, the plane's built-in self-repairing and safety maintenance systems self-healed, thus avoiding a disaster. It wasn't even a close call. How so? Thanks to the Industrial Internet of Things (IoT), smart sensors self-record and send real-time data to cloud platforms, enabling machines such as airplanes, gas turbines, and other remote machinery to self-heal before serious mishaps and safety disruptions develop.[6]

How incredulous are these scenarios? Not as far-fetched as people may think; in fact, many are already happening. The news is mostly good; no cause for alarm or fear of losing your wits or health running out of supplies. Thanks to big data and artificial intelligence (AI), machine and deep learning algorithms, 3D printing, robotics, the IoT, blockchain technology, cloud computing, and a host of supercomputing digital innovations, interconnected systems work seamlessly to better serve our needs. Fusing advanced technological products and services that integrate digital, biological, and physical aspects we're all living in the thick of—that many of us are clueless about. The caveat is, we're unprepared, let alone accept the undeniable fact we're living within the multidimensions of a Fourth Industrial Revolution. In truth, ignorance is not bliss; it prevents us from prevailing upon amazing digital benefits to facilitate daily living.

This current evolution is truly game-changing, gifting us newer technologies that are safer and more convenient to utilize. For instance, an estimated 10 million autonomous self-driving cars will be on the road by 2020. Researchers from the University of Illinois at Urbana-Champaign from various departments—engineering, robotics, control theory, traffic flow theory, cyber-physical systems, and transportation—collaborated to create an autonomous or self-driving car. Findings showed the driverless vehicle, along with twenty human-driven cars, helped human drivers reduce unnecessary accelerating and braking, plus reduced fuel consumption by 40 percent. At issue are human drivers who are more prone to erratic driving and unable to maintain a consistent speed for safe driving. This study remarkably found that just one driverless car mitigates traffic congestion and safer driving.[7]

Autonomous vehicles are already driving traffic changes on numerous private property roads. On Santa Clara University (SCU) campus in southern Silicon Valley, California's oldest institution of higher learning founded in 1851 a year before statehood, SCU's autonomous vehicles (built by Auro Robotics; auro.ai) reduced operating costs by 40–60 percent. Slower moving, self-driving shuttles on private grounds have also reduced air pollution, enhanced landscape aesthetics, and removed the need for excessive parking lots.[8] While not quite public transportation just yet, other companies such as Tesla, Google, Uber, and Apple are testing self-driving vehicles from cars to coaches for public roads.

As it is, we're just now getting comfortable integrating computer technology from the Third Industrial Revolution into our daily lives with desktop computers, laptops, and smartphones (and wondering how we managed before, when these items were nonexistent). Most people are unaware how quickly this latest Fourth Industrial Revolution has descended on us, along with ramifications affecting jobs and lifestyles. Revolutionary supercomputing forces impact our lives more rapidly, forcefully, and wondrously than the Third Industrial Revolution (and in the process, raising issues of safety,

**"It's okay if you're not wearing a body camera ...
I have satellite footage of the entire traffic stop."**

Figure 4.1. Source: ©Cartoon Resource.

privacy concerns, and productivity). How will businesses respond? How will workforce trends shake out? How can individuals *prepare now* to reap career planning benefits, to cope emotionally, to find job satisfaction?

What Is the Fourth Industrial Revolution?

Professor Klaus Schwab, founder and executive chair of the World Economic Forum held every year in Davos, Switzerland, since 1971, launched the global dialog in 2016 to recognize the Fourth Industrial Revolution and its implications with a book of the same title.[9] Schwab urges us to get used to an even more amazing and significant technological era already swirling around us, to learn how to keep up with myriad rapid changes brought on by super digital computing and the incredibly exponential speed in implementing innovations.

It's a world characterized by "extreme automation and connectedness" harnessing advanced IT technologies that are currently affecting world economies on massive scales, be it transportation, supply chain systems, agriculture, or basic human services such as healthcare and education. It bears repeating such extreme conditions necessitate our need to get ahead of the curve to carve out career choices that matter, for personal and professional advancement.

"In the new world, it is not the big fish which eats the small fish, it's the fast fish which eats the slow fish," Schwab explains.[10] With phenomenally improved supercomputing capabilities constantly evolving, this era is—totally, disruptive. Disruptive forces become overwhelming because people are unprepared. People are flummoxed, wondering what to do, and how to plan to meet these changes head on, in meaningful and satisfying ways. For example, you could start by asking: now that I'm aware of the Fourth Industrial Revolution and its impact, how will I prepare to live a more purposeful, happy, and fruitful life—personally and professionally?

Second, because technological changes are never isolated phenomena, this revolution occurs within the entire world ecosystem—not only in one country (as was also the case during the Third Industrial Revolution with galloping globalization). Far-reaching impacts on individuals, businesses, environment and sustainability, economic growth, security, education, healthcare, and other sectors are operating at every moment. For example, cybersecurity intrusions from hackers based in other countries wreak havoc with our personal information submitted online, stealthily stealing our data from filing taxes to insurance claims. Which means, "If one thing changes—or is changing constantly, as in the case of technology—the whole system needs to change to keep up," Schwab warns. Yet, we're not ready, let alone prepared or know how, to meet such demanding challenges.

Third, Schwab observes the tech revolution is not simply changing how we work and do things. Instead, as individuals, we're being changed by technology in how we perceive the world. As proof, he cites how the Internet has changed the notion of privacy for younger generations compared to their parents. Industries and people will feel the impact of this Fourth Industrial Revolution in numerous and different ways.

In previous eras, money and natural resources drove industrial revolutions. From 1784, the First Industrial Revolution used steam power for mechanical production. From 1870 on, mass manufacturing depended upon electrical energy. Electronics and the Internet took off from the 1970s for the Third Revolution.

The Fourth Industrial Revolution is different, with a major emphasis on brain energy. People with keen imagination, innovation, and drive—who, while not all the time knowing what the best recourse or actions might be in the face of numerous unknowns—try to keep up with disruptive technologies harnessing ever-increasing speeds of supercomputing power. The implication is, as super new technologies make old jobs obsolete, people must sharpen their career skills with ingenuity and willpower in their determination to succeed, and waking up to facing surprising new changes.

Schwab warns that change, especially rapid-fire change, is scary for most people, who turn away from accepting the need to meet them headlong. However, meeting change with the proper positive attitude can benefit people with new opportunities. "To learn new things, to rethink tired processes and to improve the way we work. The technological revolution has only just begun, and the transformations it will bring are a cause not just for excitement, but for hope," Schwab cheers on.[11] (Note: Schwab proposed these ideas in February 2015, before his book published.)

Implications of the Fourth Industrial Revolution

Schwab presented these notable highlights from his book on the Fourth Industrial Revolution at the 2016 World Economic Forum, January 20–23. His observations are useful guideposts for us to be aware of what these implications portend. How we, as jobseekers, employers, educational and business leaders, policy-makers, and our families can start preparing and staking out our individual approaches to accept, learn to expertly work with, and enhance our lives during this newest digital–biological–physical era (that is so swiftly superseding the previous digital revolution that had only just begun in the 1970s).

Three salient talking points emerge from Schwab's 2016 world forum introduction to the Fourth Industrial Revolution. First, and unwittingly, supercomputers have become our resource partners for enhanced and safer living, instead of our simply looking upon and using them as work tools. Second, in essence, every newer industrial revolution pushes us onto the path for lifelong learning (similar to "publish or perish" in academia), a reality where even sharks must swim to survive. Third, like all revolutions, this latest one generates both promises and perils to watch out, as Schwab cautions.[12]

However, Schwab points out that just as disruptive are severe implications wrought by this latest seismic shift of a global industrial revolution—if people are unprepared to meet the challenges. The first impact is everyone in all sectors of the economy, private and public, will feel the impact. Owing to the rapid speed, scope, and systems impact of supercomputing forces collaborating in all areas of society, the effects felt will be more intense and immediate than ever before.

Making his case, Schwab compares 1990 Detroit with 2014 Silicon Valley where the three largest corporations in two different eras earned almost the same revenues, $250 billion for Detroit and $247 billion for Silicon

Figure 4.2. Source: ©Cartoon Resource.

Valley. (No corporate names given, but inferences are clear.) However, Silicon Valley's market capitalization (or market value in terms of traded stocks) was three times higher at $1.09 trillion, against Detroit's $36 billion. Silicon Valley also employed ten times fewer employees (137,000) compared to Detroit's 1.2 million assembly-line workers.[13]

This glaring example of how exponentially easier it is to get rich today compared to a mere 25 years ago (during the Third Industrial Revolution) comes from harnessing the superpower abilities of digital technology and extreme automation characterized by quantum speed, capacities, and resources. Evidently, a company making software apps requires less capital outlay and infrastructure, thus scaling more profitably and quickly with ongoing productivity, in reducing marginal costs required to produce an item. Contrast these processes to a labor-intensive auto-manufacturing facility requiring capital outlays for space, storage, and other factory overheads. Not so secret a recipe at all, for minting millionaire and billionaire tech titans within a shorter timeframe.[14]

With super machines crunching at and spewing out big data, refining on repeated self-learning algorithms for smart and deep learning results with neural networks similar to the human brain's, plus robots fast replacing human workers, low-skilled labor is very quickly displaced. This results in a vastly smaller pocket of upper echelon brain-powered workers reaping the benefits and perks of higher wages, essentially becoming the 1 percent of elites. This trend of course further divides society into the "haves" and the "have-nots," resulting in social dissatisfaction and dysfunctional unrest for the rest of society.

One study estimated 47 percent of American jobs are at risk of becoming automated and displacing workers. Compounding this situation is the even greater displacement of mid-level skilled workers—a new phenomenon in the workplace placing the middle class at risk. This new trend displaces professionals such as accountants, real estate agents, insurance adjusters, travel agents, stockbrokers, and delivery drivers (recall the example in the introduction citing drone deliveries instead of, say, UPS or Fedex delivery personnel?), and indisputably disrupting labor markets disproportionately.

This development can take on volatile undertones. Where the myth is, professionals can easily pick up and reenter other well-paying jobs. But can they really, without retooling skills, coupled with the purposeful mindset needed to overcome obstacles while tackling new challenges, and learning new processes?[15]

Along with economic inequality and dissatisfaction experienced by the majority, how can leaders and policy-makers retain the spirit of humanity? Justin Welby, Archbishop of Canterbury, England, who attended his first Davos forum in 2016, reminded people to remember the spiritual, "This is not just about money, it is about what it is to be human."[16] (In a similar vein is Steve Jobs' vision of keeping digital users happy with functional beauty, with his spiritual strategy noted in the previous chapter on the Third Industrial Revolution—and key to Apple's prosperity and longevity.)

The question of addressing values with compassion and understanding is a tough call. Given varied and subjective interpretations held by disparate sectors and stakeholders, it is nonetheless important to consider and implement thoughtfully, to better harness digital technologies to benefit as many people as possible.

The overriding implication is clear. Not only in waking up individuals—but also shaking up industries and firms to do business differently. How can people become aware of these deeper seismic shifts, fissuring faults, and earth-shaking reverberations of the Fourth Industrial Revolution? To become proactive and better prepared emotionally to meet these challenges with lifelong learning and upskilling, appropriately retool skill sets, and to move on bravely. How can people accept ever-new innovative supercomputing technologies of this current epochal era as vital for attaining peace of mind and prosperous living?

In a July 2017 report *Fortune* pointed out the need for professionals to pursue STEM (Science, Technology, Engineering, and Math) is imperative—yet fewer women are in these professions today compared to the 1980s.[17] Why are fewer women pursuing STEM careers, and what can be done to reverse this trend, to increase gender parity in all measures in the workplace? How adaptable, flexible, and mentally agile are we in accepting constant workplace displacements and career changes as the new norm? (We discuss the need for proactive and practical education policies and higher education programs, with upskilling, in later chapters.)

Impact on Industries

What phenomenal forces do industries encounter, while flying in the face of extreme automation and interconnectedness, and operating on global platforms? Consider our discussion earlier of the three largest corporations in

Detroit 1990 with Silicon Valley's top three companies in 2014. Both generated almost similar revenues—but required 10 times more labor for Detroit, while Silicon Valley garnered over three times the market valuation topping a trillion dollars. This comparison shows how vital it is for firms with growth potential to be constantly driven, to keep on innovating ahead of competition, to scale with agility while reducing marginal costs of production, and to come out ahead profitably, thus resulting in a higher valuation compared to other firms.

Essentially, the bottom line remains the same for all industrial revolutions. "Business leaders and senior executives need to understand their changing environment, challenge the assumptions of their operating teams, and relentlessly and continuously innovate," Schwab observes.[18] The implication is clear: businesses must constantly examine and reexamine how they conduct business, to stay ahead of competition. Schwab's vision recognizes disparate digital innovations of extreme automation and connectivity as the Fourth Industrial Revolution.

Schwab explains why businesses must stay relevant, to stay ahead in the current industrial revolution. At the heart of all economies are customers, the backbone of consumerism. Businesses produce physical products and services to ultimately serve and benefit customers. With enhanced physical and digital capabilities, these items achieve a higher value placed on them. New technologies further enhance these assets with durability and resilience, even as data analytics are transforming how these assets are maintained (e.g., in the case of self-healing aircraft).

Such a widespread diffusion of innovative technologies moreover necessitates new ways of collaborating among producers and end-users. Therefore, with new technologies and multi-global platforms emerging, the impact of the Fourth Industrial Revolution on industries means old ways of doing business become less valid—with the need for businesses to keep examining and evaluating operations, production, and marketing to remain valid in a constantly evolving and changing world arena characterized by extreme automation and connectivity.

Thus, Schwab sees the effects on businesses during this latest industrial revolution as four-fold: "on customer expectations, on product enhancement, on collaborative innovation, and on organizational forms." In conversations with CEOs and business leaders around the world, Schwab finds even brilliant leaders are stumped because the unknown drivers of innovation are constantly surprising them. Such unknown forces are hard to understand and to anticipate—even for those who are the most informed and connected. Here lies another caveat, of hidden challenges to surmount, even for leaders ostensibly ahead of this era's disruptive curve.

The reason being, industries are constantly experiencing disruptions from newer supply chain systems that provide more value, thus decreasing the value of existing systems that are usually older and less nimble to adapt. Disruption for older firms comes from newer agile, growth-directed firms providing better value with quality goods at lower costs, and with faster, more creative modes of deliveries.

On the demand side, companies must adapt to consumer demands for transparency, customer engagement, and newer patterns of consumer behavior that are increasingly more dependent on mobile networks and big data analytics. Most notably, constantly reinvented and newer platforms (such as Amazon's Prime Air drone delivery service) are incessantly disrupting older, more established businesses with the way products and services are designed, produced, marketed, and delivered.[19] Many larger, established corporations have yet to unlearn older cumbersome ways of doing business—to compete successfully with digitally enhanced super technical platforms like Amazon.

Yet, given the crossroads that we are now at, there has never been a better opportunity to reflect upon "the promise and potential peril" brought on by the Fourth Industrial Revolution, Schwab exhorts. "In the end, it all comes down to people and values. We need to shape a future that works for all of us by putting people first and empowering them." Schwab's ultimate vision is to integrate the best of human nature—creativity, empathy, and stewardship—to lift humanity into a collectively shared sense of destiny.[20]

Vint Cerf (mentioned in the previous chapter as cocreator of the Internet when he led the team of scientists in the 1970s–1980s developing the U.S. Pentagon's ARPANET for sharing research data with scientists around the world) says artists are needed along with techies. Cerf enjoys science fiction because it stretches the mind's boundaries, in thinking about implications. "It teaches me that when you're inventing something you should try to think about what the consequences might be."[21]

Laura Sydell, who interviewed Cerf among other visionaries for NPR, agrees. She observes, "Our tech entrepreneurs are focused almost exclusively on how their devices will be used by individuals—not how those devices will change society. They want to make things that are addictive and entertaining. That is why I've started to take science fiction more seriously."[22] Human nature hasn't changed much, a fact that artists recognize, regardless of fancy new tools dished up by technological inventions, Sydell concluded.

"I think we can say that this market is wide open."

Figure 4.3. Source: ©Cartoon Resource.

Remarkably, in reflecting the speed of digital innovations a year later in 2017, after dialog on the Fourth Industrial Revolution began, a study conducted by the World Economic Forum and Accenture (a global consulting firm; accenture.com) projected positive results for humanity. In the next ten years, as much as 60 percent of the estimated $100 trillion value will benefit society and the environment, compared to 40 percent for businesses. In India, digital solutions are estimated to remedy financial support for underfunded small businesses valued at $410 billion while creating five million jobs. Furthermore, 94 percent of a potential $1.2 trillion value will benefit Indian society, not business shareholders. In the United Kingdom, consumers could save $25 billion in insurance and related costs for driver assistance systems, with road fatalities declining 9 percent each year, from using enhanced vehicle safety mechanisms.[23]

Value-driven results from this study will matter to CEOs aiming to steer their companies competitively—from utilizing digital technologies with useful consumer benefits such as protecting customer privacy—not just from amassing profits and growth. "For example, by addressing the United Nations' Sustainable Development Goals that combat poverty, inequality and climate change, new technologies could unlock $9 trillion of economic benefits. The challenge is that profit incentives for environmental and social investments are often weak and payback times are far longer than today's digital business models allow. As a result, much of this value to society will remain trapped."[24] The digital conundrum continues to intrigue.

Impact on Jobs

Fortuitously though, "The future is not preordained by machines. It's created by humans," declares Erik Brynjolfsson, director of MIT's Initiative on the Digital Economy. He offers three suggestions for teenagers wondering about career planning in the Fourth Industrial Revolution. First, "You want to do things machines can't do well. You want to be working with them, not competing with them," Brynjolfsson advises, where a school's creative arts curriculum helps students balance out their interests (but sadly, arts curricula are phased out in many schools, he notes). Second, acquiring emotional intelligence is important—to learn interpersonal skills, teamwork, and leadership. Tongue in cheek, he cautions, "It doesn't help to have a robot give you a pep talk." Third, "The people who do well do so because they are the best in something," Brynjolfsson notes.[25]

Seek out your passion. As the saying goes, do what you love and love what you do. Putting love, heart, and soul into what you do will give you that driving edge to excel, putting you head and shoulders above other less motivated people.

Take for example, high school sophomore Brittany Wenger, who was devastated by her cousin's breast cancer because it was hard to correctly diagnose early; she determined to help other women mitigate their trauma. Wenger created a test to catch the disease early, which now tests correctly with 99.9 percent accuracy. It all started with having to write a term paper on anything the future held, she said. She Googled what would happen fifty, a hundred years out. AI jumped out at her. She bought a textbook on coding and taught herself to computer code. The rest is her historic story, with her passion extending in developing diagnostic apps for other diseases as well, such as leukemia and diabetes.

Wenger says, "Find your passion, just follow it and have the persistence to stick through it. I mean, for me, the breast cancer program failed completely two times before it succeeded. But what's great about science is that you learn a lot from those experiments. They can really help you move forward."[26] Truly, failures are pillars to successes.

This Grand Prize Winner of the 2012 Google Science Fair Award was then only seventeen. Brittany Wenger's diagnostic health app harnesses cloud computing where doctors can access huge datasets to compare and evaluate the possibility of breast cancer cells using a minimally invasive procedure—with almost 100 percent accuracy.[27]

And while the stark reality of job losses looms for low-skill and mid-skill workers, Brynjolfsson is optimistic because cognitive computing opportunities are exploding, such as deep learning and neural networks where computers can diagnose cancer better than humans, and as a catalyst for safer autonomous driving compared to humans. And yes, education and reorientation programs acknowledging the importance of STEM and related areas are valuable for young and old to speed up and better meet job requirements for the Fourth Industrial Revolution.

Tracey's Transition Tips

In 1992 I was laid off after five years at Apple, the same year I published my first book, *Doing Business with Japanese Men: A Woman's Handbook* (Stone Bridge, 1993). The book was popular because of unknowns then, working with Japanese men. It was based off my MBA thesis as I commuted to Japan regularly, while working for Apple. John Sculley (then Apple CEO) provided a book cover quote.

Apple's continued layoffs (the dark period) had an impact on Silicon Valley. There was a constant flow of people looking for jobs—with none to be found. Thousands of people were out of work in Silicon Valley in the mid-1990s. Some people left the workforce all together; some traveled and decided to wait it out. I could not afford not to work, so I forged ahead.

I continued working on my second book, *Asia for Women on Business: Hong Kong, Taiwan, Singapore, and South Korea* (Stone Bridge, 1995); and Indra Nooyi (Chair and CEO of PepsiCo at time of this writing) provided a notable cover quote. I went on a media and speaking tour for my first book and focused on finding a job. Within months, Hewlett Packed hired me in 1993. Even though I was jobless, I negotiated a 22 percent pay raise. They hired me because I had worked for Apple, with international business experience, and had an MBA.

- Layoffs and transitions are economic events, and often lead to better opportunities. Apply for unemployment, mourn briefly, and move on. Use outplacement services offered by the firm (if they do not offer, ask for it). Focus on your next move. Remain positive.

- People hire people. Networking still accounts for the majority of job hires. Hiring managers do look at referrals from employees as strong candidates. I was referred to HP by a current employee. Tap into your network to learn about job openings at their firms. Join a professional association in your industry; meet with recruiters.

- Being laid off is not the time to change careers. If you're looking to rejoin the job market quickly, pursue the same position you had in your previous organization. The position HP hired me for had been the same at Apple.

- Know your worth and negotiate the market salary (not what you've been getting). People are often locked into a salary range when they stay for a period of time that's lower than market rate. Research current salary surveys (professional associations and recruiters) and websites (salary.com; glassdoor.com); understand your worth in the current marketplace.

- If you're in a transition period, stay active. Had I been working, I'd not have been able to go on a book tour, respond to speaking requests, or work on my second book. These activities elevated my brand and made me more employable, although I was not formally working in a company.

Notes

1. Hamish McRae, "Davos 2016: Forget the Markets—the Fourth industrial Revolution is Here," *Independent*, January 23, 2016. http://www.independent.co.uk/voices/davos-2016-forget-the-markets-the-fourth-industrial-revolution-is-here-a6830491.html.

2. Maxine Wally, "Hear This, 2017: Scientists are Creating New Ears with 3D-Printing and Human Stem Cells," *Smithsonian.com*, December 30, 2016, https://www.smithsonianmag.com/science-nature/3d-printed-ears-grown-stem-cells-are-finally-on-their-way-180961605/.

3. Clare Scott, "University of California San Diego's 3D Printed Liver Tissue may be the Closest We've Gotten to a Real Printed Liver," *3DPrint.com*, February 9, 2016, https://3d-print.com/118932/uc-san-diego-3d-printed-liver/.

4. Rob Stein, "Scientists Precisely Edit DNA in Human Embryos to Fix a Disease Gene," NPR.org, August 2, 2017, https://www.npr.org/sections/health-shots/2017/08/02/540975224/scientists-precisely-edit-dna-in-human-embryos-to-fix-a-disease-gene.

5. Luke Johnson, "9 Things You Need to Know about Amazon Prime Air Drone Delivery Service," *Digital Spy*, February 7, 2017, www.digitalspy.com/tech/feature/a820748/amazon-prime-air-drone-delivery-service/.

6. *GE Imagination at Work*, https://www.ge.com/digital/blog/prevent-evolve-profit-future-field-services.

7. "A Single Autonomous Car has a Huge Impact on Alleviating Traffic," *Mechanized Intelligence*, May 18, 2017, https://mechanizedintelligence.com/2017/05/18/a-single-autonomous-car-has-a-huge-impact-on-alleviating-traffic/.

8. Tekla S. Perry, "Auro Robotics' autonomous vehicle is shuttling students, faculty, and visitors around Santa Clara University," https://spectrum.ieee.org/view-from-the-valley/transportation/self-driving/autonomous-shuttle-brakes-for-squirrels-skateboarders-and-texting-students.

9. Klaus Schwab, *The Fourth Industrial Revolution* (New York: Crown Business, 2017).

10. Klaus Schwab, "Are you ready for the technological revolution?" World Economic Forum, February 19, 2015, https://www.weforum.org/agenda/2015/02/are-you-ready-for-the-technological-revolution/.

11. Ibid.

12. Klaus Schwab, "The Fourth Industrial Revolution: what it means, how to respond," World Economic Forum, January 14, 2016, https://www.weforum.org/agenda/2016/01/the-fourth-industrial-revolution-what-it-means-and-how-to-respond/.

13. Larry Elliott, "Fourth Industrial Revolution brings promise and peril for humanity," the *Guardian*, January 24, 2016, https://www.theguardian.com/business/economics-blog/2016/jan/24/4th-industrial-revolution-brings-promise-and-peril-for-humanity-technology-davos.

14. Ibid. Andrew Berg, "Revolution Evolution," IMF Book Review, December 2016, https://www.imf.org/external/pubs/ft/fandd/2016/12/book3.htm.

15. Ibid. Also noted in *UBS White Paper on the Fourth Industrial Revolution*, https://www.ubs.com/global/en/about_ubs/follow_ubs/highlights/davos-2016.html.

16. Larry Elliott, "Fourth Industrial Revolution brings promise and peril for humanity," the *Guardian*, January 24, 2016, https://www.theguardian.com/business/economics-blog/2016/jan/24/4th-industrial-revolution-brings-promise-and-peril-for-humanity-technology-davos.

17. Valentina Zarya, "Here's What the Highest-Paid Female CEOs Have in Common," *Fortune*, June 20, 2017, fortune.com/2017/06/20/female-fortune-500-ceo/.

18. Klaus Schwab, "The Fourth Industrial Revolution: what it means, how to respond," World Economic Forum, January 14, 2016, https://www.weforum.org/agenda/2016/01/the-fourth-industrial-revolution-what-it-means-and-how-to-respond/.

19. Ibid.

20. Ibid.

21. Laura Sydell, "The Father of the Internet Sees His Invention Reflected Back through a 'Black Mirror'," NPR.org, February 20, 2018, https://www.npr.org/sections/alltechconsidered/2018/02/20/583682937/the-father-of-the-internet-sees-his-invention-reflected-back-through-a-black-mir.

22. Ibid.

23. Pierre Nanterme, "The Real Value of the Fourth Industrial Revolution? The Benefit to Society," January 17, 2017, World Economic Forum, https://www.weforum.org/agenda/2017/01/the-real-value-of-the-fourth-industrial-revolution-the-benefit-to-society/.

24. Ibid.

25. World Economic Forum, "Jobs and the Fourth Industrial Revolution," January 19, 2017, https://www.weforum.org/about/jobs-and-the-fourth-industrial-revolution.

26. Brooke Borel, "This College Freshman is a Cancer Detective: A Q&A with Brittany Wenger," IDEAS.TED.COM, December 12, 2013, https://ideas.ted.com/brittany-wenger-cancer-research/.

27. Cristin Frodella, "The Winners of the 2012 Google Science Fair," July 23, 2012, https://www.blog.google/topics/education/the-winners-of-2012-google-science-fair/.

SECTION II

FORCES IMPACTING YOUR CAREER AND EMPLOYABILITY

· 5 ·

HOW KEY MEGATRENDS OF CHANGE IMPACT ORGANIZATIONS AND CAREERS

Along with the Third and Fourth Industrial Revolutions elevating businesses and individuals to stratospheric heights of digital innovations and productivity in less than half a century compared to the first two industrial revolutions spanning two hundred years, this chapter discusses other key forces forcing sea changes disrupting organizations and employment patterns, and career planning for individuals today. No country is exempt from these changing scenarios; neither are individuals and the businesses they serve. Every local and global economy has to keep up with change, regardless of whether they want to, or are prepared to do so.

In large part, such seismic forces are the result of digital innovations dishing up extreme automation and connectivity that even many top CEOs are stymied not knowing how to meet them head on.[1] This is because the rate of change continues to accelerate exponentially, dotted with myriad unknown variables (many positive, some less so), in affecting the scope and extent of ecosystems simultaneously, both at home and abroad. However, other socio-economic factors are also at work giving rise to serious megatrends, which are not static and continue evolving.

What are megatrends? The Hay Group defines megatrends not as fads, but powerful movements or paradigm shifts exhibiting three key characteristics.

First, current empirical socioeconomic–business data can project scenarios with a high degree of probability for planning purposes, at least fifteen years out. Second, megatrends affect all levels of ecosystems—government, businesses, and individuals. Third, megatrends affect every fundamental and multidimensional subsystem and substrata of ecosystems with their systemic impact, thus giving rise to precise features that are unique to each region.[2] This chapter examines four leading social and economic megatrends that are impacting world regions today.

First, with quality of life vastly enhanced by advanced technologies in the medical and life sciences, air and road transportation safety, drone deliveries obviating driving to stores in sprawling suburbia, plus other life-saving enhancements, we're given the tools to live not only longer, but also to enjoy life with better health and fitness. However, today's human longevity means introducing new issues, such as individuals having to work longer and for more years, to adroitly plan for affordable retirement,[3] and for organizational leaders to learn how to harmoniously and productively manage five generations in the same workplace.[4]

Second, pervasive globalization prodded on by digital automation and connectivity creates a much more competitive environment for organizations to survive, let alone thrive productively. This of course puts pressure on organizations to hire, develop, and retain competitive leaders and employees who are globally savvy, who feel comfortable in working with diverse teams and multicultural firms. In addition, other workforce trends are emerging, such as companies hiring freelancers and contractors (very often working remotely, including offshore stringers) while lessening their dependence on in-house employees.[5]

Third, the changing contemporary family structure increases the need for flexible work options rather than slogging away at the traditional face-to-face, 9–5, workday. In reflecting another shift away from single households historically headed by poor women and minorities, single motherhood households with children under eighteen are increasingly the norm in this country. The 2017 U.S. Census Bureau reports 80 percent of single-parent U.S. households headed by women, with two-thirds under the age of thirty.[6] We'll also delve into what it means for families living the sandwich generation, where those working full-time, in addition to taking care of their kids, also take care of aging parents—some hospitalized, thus requiring long stays away from home and/or throwing another wrench into longer work commutes.[7]

The fourth megatrend literally changing the face of the local and global workforce, and even more significantly as a marker for social change, and professionally acknowledged today, is—diversity and inclusivity. According to a LinkedIn social media blog for professionals, "Diversity is the new global mindset," with 78 percent HR professionals citing this socioeconomic shift influencing how they hire. The three main reasons cited for hiring to reflect diversity are to: (a) improve company culture (78 percent); (b) improve company performance (62 percent); and (c) better represent customers (49 percent).[8]

In the United States, there is every reason for businesses to benefit when they reflect a company's customer base, with millennials (those born 1982–2004) being the most racially diverse (43 percent are nonwhite) and as well comprising the largest segment of the U.S. population to date. Millennials are also better educated, albeit a double-edged distinction. Most millennials still live at home (thus adding to the sandwich generation) because of massive student debts. However, saddled as they are with huge student loans to repay over decades (competitively compounded by the loss of many mid-skilled jobs that are now automated), the Pew Research Center nevertheless finds this generation shares a positive attitude. Eight in ten voice the optimism that they will have money later to live the life they envision.[9]

Psychologists analyzed 2017 data from the World Gallup Poll from 1.7 million people in 164 countries, scaled according to country analysis. In America, $95,000 is the ideal annual income for individuals when assessing life satisfaction in terms of how people felt they were doing. For emotional well-being, $60,000–$75,000 a year was ideal to reflect the person's happiness, sadness, excitement, or anger.[10]

We continue discussing why considering career choices early is most helpful to avoid career confusion later on for younger and older workers alike—as shifting sands of the contemporary marketplace crumple the traditional workplace model. Four megatrends are discussed separately: (a) how increasing longevity affects an aging workforce, (b) the latest wave of globalization, (c) the changing American family structure, and (d) diversity in the workforce.

How Increasing Longevity Affects an Aging Workforce

Advances in the health and life sciences enable us to live to a hundred and over today. A 2014 Merrill Lynch survey conducted with Age Wave found

81 percent retirees preferred good health to live out their bucket lists. Fifty-eight percent opted for financial security.[11]

This begs the question of whether we can afford to live a long life blessed with quality living, and spared from the indignity of living in poverty in old age. How would financial security shake out with social security, minimal and sometimes lost pensions? Even more serious an implication reveals many retirees with zero savings to fall back on.

The U.S. Census Bureau attributes this country's aging population to boomers (born 1943–1960) who have fewer children while also living longer.

Figure 5.1. Source: ©Cartoon Resource.

U.S. boomers are a special demographic category and a disproportionately larger aging group. The Federal Interagency on Aging notes that while the United States has been aging steadily during the previous century a more rapidly aging population has emerged with boomers, especially when they turn 65.[12] Boomers, so called because they were born during the baby boom generation after World War II when people felt good about having more offspring, are however having fewer children themselves.

With younger generations saddled with immense student debts and incrementally increasing costs to raise kids, population groups are leveling off after the boomer generation. Overall, the global population is aging, fast, as well. In fact, America has a younger aging population compared to countries in Europe, Asia, and Latin America.[13]

Compared to the booming 20th century, world populations have been dropping, even reversing, for this millennium. Inevitably and obviously, with an aging global population, employers need to plan ahead, to better meet projected talent shortfalls for job seekers (from those entering to those in aging cohorts) to clue in on new trends to capitalize on.

Consequently, population aging has serious socioeconomic consequences for individuals, employers, and leaders (private, public, nonprofit, government). By 2035, one in five persons will be 65 or older, creating a workforce crisis not only in America, but also around the world. According to the Boston Consulting Group, the top fifteen largest world economies will feel the most impact of aging populations, as they constitute 70 percent of global GDP.[14]

Along with an aging workforce, another urgent need is to rethink retirement systems initially designed to support people for 10–15 years upon retiring at age 60–65. Now, in the face of research showing people spending 20–25 percent more time working in retirement, with many living up to a hundred, planning for quality longevity and retirement security takes on new complexities and implications.[15]

Equally discouraging is the fact that corporate pensions are diminishing, even disappearing, according to Lynda Gratton and Andrew Scott, professors at the London School of Economics and authors of *The 100-Year Life: Living and Working in an Age of Longevity* (Bloomsbury, 2016). This corporate trend leaves workers having to scramble to save more while still working, to afford decent retirement incomes. Yet, the irony in the face of disappearing corporate pensions surfaces blatantly when corporations expect to tap into an estimated $15 trillion worth of spending power generated by those over age 65, these authors point out.[16]

Authors Gratton and Scott urge corporations to view older workers as assets, not liabilities—to rethink the workforce paradigm afresh, to tap into the wisdom and experience older workers bring to the table. This is an important point—for business leaders to understand and to be motivated to change nonproductive legacy thinking and mindsets. Why?

Recalibrating leadership mindsets is vital because these two authors find, "Longevity means people are living longer and staying healthier for longer." Along with a healthier older generation that is also more fit and fitness-oriented

"We're doing everything you guys did-marriage, career, children-only in reverse."

Figure 5.2. Source: ©Cartoon Resource.

to live healthily compared to previous ones, current older workers are even more productive when augmented with technological advancements, the authors found.[17]

Another study also bucks previous theories postulating an aging population produces "secular stagnation" due to lowered productivity from an older labor force, and/or the elderly preferring to hold on to savings instead of investing their monies. A 2017 study by the National Bureau of Economic Research (nber.org) shows countries with rapidly aging populations generate a counterintuitive effect with faster economic growth happening in tandem with adopting automation technologies.[18] The bottom line is, with people experiencing longevity and staying healthy and fit longer, decades of learning insights and career churns do add value and worth to enhancing workplace productivity—as older generations of workers currently exemplify.

It bears repeating, "The future is not preordained by machines. It's created by humans," asserts Erik Brynjolfsson, director at MIT's Initiative on the Digital Economy.[19] Why would forward-looking successful corporations not want to harness the wisdom of aging workforce generations? As these studies show, the newer and smarter trend in recombining a wisely aging workforce with automation enhances a firm's overall efforts to reimagine and predict the future more sustainably and fruitfully.

Noticeably, according to the Strauss-Howe generational theory, workplace compositions increasingly reflect five levels of age groups[20]:

1) Silent Generation, born 1925–1942
2) Boomers, born 1943–1960
3) Generation X, born 1961–1981
4) Generation Y (millennials), born 1982–2004
5) Generation Z, born 2005 and on

Combining all five generational levels within one workplace of course presents unprecedented challenges to workforce managers. Business leaders must be open to developing experiential learning on the job to promote harmony and productivity. How does a firm's company culture promote and develop methodologies to transfer deep knowledge from older generations to incoming, younger generations?

This new trend of working within a five-generational workforce invariably opens up other career opportunities, too—for instance, people with expertise training diverse teams to communicate and understand each other, plus knowing how to motivate and retain top talent. A vision not quite impossible for industries be they healthcare, education, or computing—for a "mission-critical skill" fast trending as a skillset vital to drive company performance, for companies to keep on innovating seamlessly to come out ahead of competition.[21]

Globalization

Research studies cited thus far explain the numerous significant implications brought on by extreme automation and connectivity driven by technological inventions. No one is left out with digital industrial revolutions impacting everyone, everywhere, even nomadic tribes in the sub-Saharan Desert—which highlights another megatrend. Enter "Globalization 2.0" and how it impacts the world economy as explained by two authors from the Hay Group.

Georg Vielmetter and Yvonne Sell, authors of Leadership 2030 (AMACOM, 2014), explain why Globalization 2.0 is not a fad. In later decades of the 20th century, globalization saw developed countries outsourcing production (e.g., manufacturing) and services (e.g., customer service call centers) to countries with lower costs of production. Outsourcing brought cost savings to businesses in more developed economies (and a dominant trend throughout history).

However, a newer iteration of globalization patterns resulting from clusters of innovation, manufacturing, and population centers—with China on track to surpass the United States as the world's largest economy—is heralding yet newer versions of globalization in upending older models of world trade. Vielmetter and Sell define Globalization 2.0 as a new economic world order of a megatrend, wherein centers of power shift from historically developed economies in the West to fast-developing markets in Asia, especially China. As was the case for developed economies, the rise of the middle class in emerging markets and centers of power is not only imminent, it is already happening.[22]

In earlier first and second industrial revolutions, trade routes predominantly connected Europe to the Americas (excluding slave-trading hubs that connected Africa and Asia with Latin America). Today, a McKinsey Global Institute publication explains, global trade systems have morphed into complex and intricate connections. Asia (where two of the world's largest populations reside, China and India, each with over a billion people) is now the leading region for world trade and bustling economic hubs. For example,

"Can you tell me what the competition
is planning in the next quarter?"

Figure 5.3. Source: ©Cartoon Resource.

and significantly, trade volume between China and Africa increased over twenty-three times in just twelve years, from $9 billion in 2000 to $211 billion in 2012. China is on the verge of overtaking America as the next largest economy[23] (also noted by other researchers previously cited). By 2025, McKinsey forecasts China will be home to more large companies, rather than America and Europe.

In going global, technology-enabled firms of course make faster headway. From analyzing thousands of companies around the world, another McKinsey Global Institute report found three common traits in tech-enabled firms. First, intellectual assets with continuous innovative research and development are heavy areas of strategic investment for these tech-reliant firms. Continuous innovation puts them ahead in anticipating the future. Second, tech-empowered firms readily expand their spread and outreach in rapidly growing markets and regions, such as quickly growing population centers in Asia, Africa, and Latin America. Third, not surprisingly, tech-enabled firms manifest the most efficient operations (and because of technology, often cost savings, too)—all adding to more lucrative profits for these firms.[24]

In addition, agile companies that can readily adapt to dynamic world conditions will capture more opportunities, as reflected by management and team members ably going with the ebb and flow of changing consumer and economic tides. Nimble tech-enabled firms reap enormous benefits from tapping into markets with emerging and expanding populations, spawning ever-growing newer markets of consumer demands. Digital technologies fuel innovations to keep up to speed, meeting new demands that are also culture specific to each unique region. Global competition can only get more intense for companies—to survive and to readily pounce on emerging opportunities, to forge ahead stronger than competition.[25]

Changing U.S. Family Structure

Along with galloping globalization breaking down traditional frontiers of world trade, barriers are also being broken on the home front. As we're reminded, constant change is a multidimensional effect impacting everyone, at all levels. Such as children born out of wedlock in the previous century, a social stigma that rendered millions of American babies to be put up for adoption (as was the case for Apple founder Steve Jobs, whose blood father was Syrian Abdulfattah Jandali, PhD).[26]

With the new normal for four out of ten U.S. children born out of wedlock, women increasingly head single-parent households, with two-thirds under age thirty. Given trickle-down consequences, one in four U.S. children under eighteen (17.2 million) are raised by single mothers. According to the U.S. Census Bureau, there were 11,667,000 single-parent families in 2017, with 81.7 percent headed by single mothers.[27]

Among single moms, half never married, 29 percent divorced, and 21 percent separated or widowed. Median income earned by single moms averaged $35,400 while married couples earned $85,300. Of over 10 million low-income working families in America, 4.1 million households are headed by single moms. Single-parent households are invariably economically disadvantaged, with 35.6 percent of these households living in poverty in 2016—and extremely vulnerable to homelessness for single parents and their children.[28]

Opting to stay single is trending as another new normal for Americans. According to the U.S. Census Bureau, 37.3 million remained unmarried in 1950 versus 74.4 million who were married. By 2015 (65 years later), 121.5 million persons chose to remain single compared to 133.6 million who married.[29] Single households afford more disposable incomes, thus providing incentives to stay single; also perhaps in light of staying on top of caregiving duties.

The National Alliance of Caregiving and the American Association of Retired Persons' landmark study of *Caregiving in the U.S. 2015 Final Report* estimated 43.5 million (or one out of six) Americans provided unpaid caregiving to elderly parents or disabled children. The average caregiver is a 49-year-old female looking after another 69-year-old, most likely mother; she also provides more complicated nursing-care related duties giving mother her shots, tube-feeding, catheters, and colostomy attention. Caregivers perform these duties averaging 24 hours weekly, in addition to holding at least a 35-hour to full-time workweek. A quarter of these caregivers were millennials, half as many men as women.[30]

Typically, caregivers who offer their services at least 21 hours a week have been doing it five-and-a-half years, and expect to continue at least five more years. Understandably, 46 percent say they are stressed out—emotionally, physically, and financially—especially when their annual family income averages $45,700.[31]

The primary takeaway from this study is, researchers found employers (public and private) do not give adequate support to their employee caregivers. The caveat is, this double-edged situation does not help both care recipients and employee caregivers. This unfortunate situation puts all parties at risk.[32]

Another report on this groundbreaking study adds that overall, 40 percent of caregivers are men and 60 percent women; one in ten caregivers are 75 and older; and all ethnic groups are involved. Currently, there are seven caregivers available for each recipient. But by 2050, only three caregivers are available to each recipient, owing to overall population decline.[33]

By now, it should be no surprise that the majority of American households are multigenerational—in fact, 60.6 million or 19 percent of the U.S. population in 2014, according to Pew Research Center. A multigenerational household includes at least two generations of adults. This trend increased during and after the Great Recession, 2007–2009. Increasing racial and ethnic diversity accounts for multigenerational households: 28 percent for Asian, 25 percent for African Americans and Hispanics, with 15 percent for Caucasians.[34]

It is no surprise too that with caregiving and multigenerational households taking center stage today, this latest iteration of a "sandwich generation" has evolved. Caring for children and frail parents amounts to burning both ends of the candle for these adults. About 43 percent note their careers have suffered, too. Caregivers call for more reasonable workplace adjustments— such as options to work remotely, to be evaluated on project results (instead of showing up 9–5), job sharing, and for more on-the-job flexibility—all of which have been found to reduce stress levels while enhancing productivity gains for sandwich generation employees.[35]

Clearly, workplace adjustments have to keep up with changing social demands and family patterns developing not only in America, but also around the world. Managers and team leaders need to devise fair and creative markers for job accountability based on results. Plus cultivating understanding and empathy for sandwich generation caregivers not to burn out.

As an aside, the Analysis Group cited National Institute of Mental Health findings that 18 percent of American adults suffer from major depression, costing U.S. productivity losses estimated at $210.5 billion annually. Globally, depression costs businesses $1 trillion annually in lost productivity. Sixty-two percent of U.S. and Canadian employers believe depression is prevalent in the workplace; while 68 percent today feel more challenged about mental health and substance abuse among employees compared to five years ago.[36]

Diversity and Inclusion

According to LinkedIn Talent Solutions, there are four major trends facing recruiters in 2018, and diversity is huge. (The other three are: candidate assessment tools to help identify top talent, big data, and artificial intelligence.) Dubbed "the new global mindset," diversity is the current lightning rod for recruiters; 78 percent call it "very/extremely important," and 53 percent have "mostly/completely" adopted diversity in recruiting candidates. Why? It drives the company's bottom line. It literally pays to attract employees who understand an increasingly diverse customer base—irrespective of racial, ethnic, gender, or age issues.[37]

The U.S. Census Bureau's data for 2015–2016 shows racial and ethnic population groups growing faster than non-Hispanic whites (the traditional dominant group). The top two growing segments are Asians and people of mixed race, with both groups increasing by 3 percent. Asians increased 21.4 million, while mixed-race people increased by 8.5 million. However, non-Hispanic white births were just 5,000, with higher deaths coming in at 163,300, and remaining constant at 198 million for this segment. Hispanics were the second largest ethnic group at 57.5 million, followed by blacks at 46.8 million.[38]

In a nutshell, America's growing diversity is a logical development for industries to embrace this global megatrend change for all the right employment and business reasons. The evidence is growing with diverse teams showing more productivity, from becoming engaged and innovative. Yet, many firms fall short of accomplishing this goal to hire more diversely.[39]

According to LinkedIn's Talent Solution blog, the biggest barrier to increasing diversity in the workplace is finding candidates to interview (38 percent). Other problems are retaining diverse employees (27 percent), getting diverse candidates past the interview stage (14 percent), and getting diverse candidates to accept offers (8 percent). However, companies like Walgreens and Lever get around these barriers creatively with employee resource groups, in encouraging employee expression and garnering strong executive support.[40]

Fortune magazine's annual ranking of "100 Best Companies to Work For/2018" (this ranking began in 1998) found, "Organizations that scored high on measures of inclusivity grew revenue three times as fast as rivals." Furthermore, "The key to business success is maximizing human potential, accomplished through leadership effectiveness, values, and trust. Get those pieces right, and you will see innovation and financial growth."[41]

The latest megatrend the world over clearly shows adopting diversity and inclusivity is smart business. Doing right by inculcating values that nurture humans and corporate culture pays dividends because inclusiveness accelerates business performance. Every employee matters—especially when top talent is getting scarcer, newer job requirements to meet changing workforce needs for digitally savvy workers are constantly exploding, and competition heating up even more among recruiters to place top talent.

Notes

1. Klaus Schwab, "The Fourth Industrial Revolution: what it means, how to respond," World Economic Forum, January 14, 2016, https://www.weforum.org/agenda/2016/01/the-fourth-industrial-revolution-what-it-means-and-how-to-respond/.
2. Yvonne Sell, The Hay Group, *Leadership 2030—The Future of Leadership*, March 2014, https://dif.fi/wp-content/uploads/2014/03/dif-presentation_yvonne-sell.pdf.
3. World Economic Forum White Paper, "We'll Live to 100—How Can we Afford It?" May 2017, http://www3.weforum.org/docs/WEF_White_Paper_We_Will_Live_to_100.pdf.

4. Team CGK (Center for Generational Kinetics), "Five Generations of Employees in Today's Workforce," April 27, 2015, http://genhq.com/five-generations-of-employees-in-todays-workforce/.

5. Vikram Bhalla, Susanne Drychs, & Rainer Starck, Boston Consulting Group, "Twelve Forces that Will Radically Change How Organizations Work," March 27, 2017, https://www.bcg.com/publications/2017/people-organization-strategy-twelve-forces-radically-change-organizations-work.aspx.

6. Dawn Lee, "Single Mother Statistics," January 10, 2018, *singlemotherguide.com*, https://singlemotherguide.com/single-mother-statistics/.

7. Ann Diab, "Flexible Work Strategies and the Companies That Use Them," *Fast Company*, March 30, 2016, https://www.fastcompany.com/3058344/5-flexible-work-strategies-and-the-companies-who-use-them.

8. Maria Ignatova & Kate Reilly, "The 4 Trends Changing How You Hire in 2018 and Beyond," LinkedIn Talent Blog, January 10, 2018, https://business.linkedin.com/talent-solutions/blog/trends-and-research/2018/4-trends-shaping-the-future-of-hiring.

9. D'Vera Cohn & Andrea Caumont, "10 demographic trends that are shaping the U.S. and the world," Pew Research Center, March 31, 2016, http://www.pewresearch.org/fact-tank/2016/03/31/10-demographic-trends-that-are-shaping-the-u-s-and-the-world/.

10. Quentin Fottrell, "Psychologists say they're found the exact amount of money you need to be happy," *MarketWatch*, March 1, 2018, https://www.marketwatch.com/story/this-is-exactly-how-much-money-you-need-to-be-truly-happy-earning-more-wont-help-2018-02-14.

11. Bank of America Newsroom, "Merrill Lynch Study Finds Health is the Cornerstone of a Happy Retirement, and Greatest Financial Worry," September 12, 2014, http://newsroom.bankofamerica.com/press-releases/global-wealth-and-investment-management/merrill-lynch-study-finds-health-cornerstone-.

12. Federal Interagency on Aging Related Statistics, "Population Aging in the United States," n.d., https://agingstats.gov/images/olderamericans_agingpopulation.pdf.

13. Ibid.

14. Vikram Bhalla, Susanne Drychs, & Rainer Starck, Boston Consulting Group, "Twelve Forces that Will Radically Change How Organizations Work," March 27, 2017, https://www.bcg.com/publications/2017/people-organization-strategy-twelve-forces-radically-change-organizations-work.aspx.

15. World Economic Forum White Paper, "We'll Live to 100—How Can we Afford It?" May 2017, http://www3.weforum.org/docs/WEF_White_Paper_We_Will_Live_to_100.pdf.

16. Lynda Gratton & Andrew Scott, "The Corporate Implications of Longer Lives," *MIT Sloan Management Review & Report*, April 18, 2017, https://tribunecontentagency.com/article/the-corporate-implications-of-longer-lives/.

17. Ibid.

18. Daron Acemoglu & Pascual Restrepo, "Secular Stagnation? The Effect of Aging on Economic Growth in the Age of Automation," National Bureau of Economic Research, Working Paper No. 23077, January 2017, https://www.nber.org/papers/w23077.

19. World Economic Forum, "Jobs and the Fourth Industrial Revolution," January 19, 2017, https://www.weforum.org/about/jobs-and-the-fourth-industrial-revolution.

20. https://en.wikipedia.org/wiki/Strauss–Howe_generational_theory.
21. Center for Generational Kinetics, "Five Generations of Employees in Today's Workforce, Managers and Leaders Face an Unprecedented Challenge," April 27, 2015, http://genhq.com/five-generations-of-employees-in-todays-workforce/.
22. Georg Vielmetter & Yvonne Sell, *Leadership 2030* (AMACOM, 2014).
23. Richard Dobbs, James Manyika, & Jonathan Woetzel, "The four global forces breaking all the trends," McKinsey Global Institute Book Excerpt, April 2015, https://www.mckinsey.com/business-functions/strategy-and-corporate-finance/our-insights/the-four-global-forces-breaking-all-the-trends.
24. Richard Dobbs, Tim Koller, Sree Ramaswarmy, Jonathan Woetzel, James Manyika, Rohit Krishnan, & Nicolo Andreula, "The New Global Competition for Profits," McKinsey Global Institute Report, September 2015, https://www.mckinsey.com/business-functions/strategy-and-corporate-finance/our-insights/the-new-global-competition-for-corporate-profits.
25. Ibid.
26. Walter Isaacson, *Steve Jobs* (New York: Simon & Schuster, 2011).
27. U.S. Census Bureau, "Stats for Stories: National Spouses Day," January 26, 2018, https://www.census.gov/newsroom/stories/2018/spouses.html.
28. Dawn Lee, "Single Mother Statistics," January 10, 2018, https://singlemotherguide.com/single-mother-statistics/.
29. U.S. Census Bureau, "Stats for Stories: Singles Awareness Day," February 15, 2018, https://www.census.gov/newsroom/stories/2018/singles.html.
30. National Alliance for Caregiving, "Caregiving in the U.S. 2015," http://www.caregiving.org/caregiving2015/.
31. Ibid.
32. Laura Santhanam, "Millennials make up substantial share of America's caregivers," *Nation*, June 4, 2015, https://www.pbs.org/newshour/nation/millennials-make-large-share-americas-caregivers.
33. Emily Gurnon, "Who America's Caregivers Are and Why It Matters," *NextAvenue*, June 4, 2015, https://www.nextavenue.org/who-americas-caregivers-are-and-why-it-matters/.
34. D'Vera Cohn & Jeffery S. Passel, "A record 60.6 million Americans live in multigenerational households," August 11 2016, Pew Research Center, http://www.pewresearch.org/fact-tank/2016/08/11/a-record-60-6-million-americans-live-in-multigenerational-households/.
35. Ann Diab, "5 Flexible Work Strategies and the Companies that Use Them," *Fast Company*, March 30, 2016, https://www.fastcompany.com/3058344/5-flexible-work-strategies-and-the-companies-who-use-them.
36. Etelka Lehoczky, "Keeping Your Workers Well," *Inc.*, March/April 2018, 42–44.
37. LinkedIn Talent Solutions, "Global Recruiting Trends 2018," https://business.linkedin.com/talent-solutions/recruiting-tips/2018-global-recruiting-trends?trk=bl-ba_global-recruiting-trends-launch_maria-ignatova_011018#.
38. Bill Chappell, "Census Finds a More Diverse America, as Whites Lag Growth," NPR.org, June 22, 2017, https://www.npr.org/sections/thetwo-way/2017/06/22/533926978/

census-finds-a-more-diverse-america-as-whites-lag-growth. U.S. Census Bureau Quick Facts, July 1, 2017, https://www.census.gov/quickfacts/fact/table/US/PST045217.

39. Maria Ignatova & Kate Reilly, "Global Recruiting Trends 2018," LinkedIn Talent Blog, January 10, 2018, https://business.linkedin.com/talent-solutions/blog/trends-and-research/2018/4-trends-shaping-the-future-of-hiring.

40. Ibid.

41. Michael C. Bush & Sarah Lewis-Kulin, "100 Best Companies to Work For/2018," *Fortune*, March 1, 2018, 53–78.

· 6 ·

TALENT SHORTAGE AND THE SKILLS GAP

In this heyday of global economics, America and countries the world over are facing a critical skills shortage. Study after study conducted by top research firms such as Pew Research Center, Society for Human Resource Management (SHRM), Bloomberg, McKinsey, and the World Economic Forum confirms this dire predicament faced by employers who are desperate to hire quality, good-fit employees. Job skills today are constantly evolving, even as the half-life of a learned skill becomes obsolete in five years. Currently, 6.2 million jobs in the United States remain unfilled, up from 5.6 million in 2016, notes a *Forbes* workplace trend forecast for 2018.[1]

This chapter discusses major studies on the widening skills gap affecting talent shortfalls for unfilled jobs with serious ramifications for America's overall economy, at all levels of skills, from low to higher levels of job expertise. This widening pattern of a skills gap in the U.S. labor market worries economists because it leads to reducing national productivity, thus lowering America's GDP over the long haul—especially in light of rising economies such as China's.

What skills are in demand? How can employers and employees work toward middle ground to keep up with increasing needs for enhanced productivity? What are some purposeful interventions from education and private sector policy-makers to mitigate this worsening trend?

What Is the State of Today's U.S. Job Market?

The Pew Research Center's *State of American Jobs* (October 6, 2016) and Markle Foundation surveyed 5,006 adults (both employed and unemployed) from May 25 to June 29, 2016. Important findings from this survey upended previous national employment patterns. Significantly, it showed knowledge-based jobs are currently the main driver reshaping the American workplace.

First, employment is increasing faster for jobs requiring more preparation; workers have to be articulate in social and communication skills, plus more analytical with critical thinking skills. A second major trend is for both employers and employees knowing they must focus on continuous learning with training and job reskilling, to keep up with new technological advancements (54 percent). A third major trend finds colleges need to rethink curricula, to shift from personal growth and intellectualism (35 percent), to also offer training with job-related skills (50 percent) to better prepare graduates for a highly competitive job market.[2]

Seven in ten individuals say they themselves are responsible for the education and training required for their success in today's job market. Individuals see upskilling as a personal responsibility; 45 percent were personally motivated to get extra training to improve job skills in the past year. Sixty percent feel K–12 schools are primarily responsible for their basic education. A third who feel they need more training to get ahead say on-the-job training is more relevant.

What are job skills respondents perceive as important? These call for a combination of technical and soft skills needed for job advancement. A majority of respondents (85 percent) say it's very important to have computer skills, the ability to work in a diverse workforce (85 percent), ability to write and communicate well (85 percent), and have access to upskilling and job training (82 percent).[3] In other words, worker perceptions of basic job competencies align with those of employers.

Interestingly, women who make up 47 percent of America's workforce are benefiting from this shift moving toward more analytical and social skills on the job (52 and 55 percent, respectively), with men in 70 percent of jobs requiring more physical and manual skills. This pattern has narrowed the gender pay gap from 1980 to 2015. This shift also signals the rise of a knowledge-based and service-oriented U.S. economy.

Another notable shift is the increase in freelancers and independent contractors. Along with temporary workers, an estimated 24 million Americans

Figure 6.1. Source: ©Cartoon Resource.

(15.8 percent of the workforce) work the "gig economy," finding employment through such nontraditional avenues. About half, 49 percent of respondents, are "very satisfied" with their current jobs.[4] This begs the question: what about the remaining 51 percent who would like to find well-paying jobs that satisfy them?

While the majority of Americans keep looking for fulfilling jobs that pay the bills, employers are also scanning the vast horizon of U.S. workforces for workers who make good-fit employees for the long haul. Why for the long haul? Because it costs employers money every time they have to hire someone.

According to SHRM it costs on average $4,129 to hire one individual in 2016, in addition to taking an average of 42 days to fill one vacancy. The average employee tenure is for eight years; the annual turnover rate is 19 percent, with an annual involuntary turnover rate at 8 percent. Sixty-one percent of employers offer tuition reimbursement, with $4,000 as the average annual payout to an employee. As an aside, annual salary increases averaged 2.7 percent, averaging 10.2 percent for executives and 4.7 percent for nonexecutives.[5]

That's why employers are always on the lookout for good-fit talent they can retain, and for longer. However, companies around the world are facing an ever-widening skills gap with potential hires lacking the requisite tools in order to be hired. What are some major issues bugging the growing skills gap?

Regional Skills Gaps Have Unique Needs

While the debate on talent shortage and skills gaps may give the impression that this is a national dilemma, in reality it is less homogeneous. In Lesley Hirsch's view, "The national skills gap is a fallacy notion, because there's no national labor market. There are regional labor markets," notes the director of New York City Labor Market Information Service. These pockets of regional labor markets have their own needs and available workers.[6]

For example, in 2015, 59 percent of Oregon's employers found it hard to fill jobs. Their three top challenges were not enough applicants had applied to job openings, a lack of qualified applicants, and unfavorable working conditions. In Texas, also in 2015, with 55 percent job vacancies, employers said applicants lacked relevant work experience, applicants turned down their offers, and applicants lacked soft skills such as dependability and problem-solving skills. In 2016, employers in North Carolina found it hard to fill 39 percent of job vacancies because applicants lacked work experience, education, certification or training, and technical skills.[7]

Other work-related issues include prevailing company and community cultures. For instance, management who do not listen to input from low-level employees breed low morale experienced by current and former employees. One worker said if employees felt they were valued, they would stick around longer. Working mother households would benefit from access to transportation and childcare. Another example of how integrated and widespread employment issues have become is for employers to rethink the traditional paradigm of recruiting farm kids (who have become scarcer) and to extend hiring to women for manufacturing and construction companies. Also, integrate underemployed newer immigrants into the community from countries such as Somalia and Sudan, while helping them assimilate economically and socially.[8]

Impact of a Widening Skills Gap

In an online survey conducted with Harris Poll, a 2016–2017 CareerBuilder study found two in three employers (67 percent) worried about the mounting skills gap (note, this is a growing phenomenon). Why are employers worried?

Because more than half (55 percent) see negative repercussions impacting their businesses from widening skills gaps on:

- Productivity losses at 45 percent
- A higher employee turnover at 40 percent
- Lower morale among workers, 39 percent
- Resulting in lower quality work, 37 percent
- Unable to grow their businesses, 29 percent
- Revenue losses, 26 percent[9]

Obviously, losses in productivity (45 percent) translate into revenue losses (26 percent) for these businesses surveyed. The consequences are especially dire because companies are in highly competitive markets to: (a) survive, (b) hire top talent, and (c) continue thriving lucratively long term from reaping increasing profits.

"My skills travel well."

Figure 6.2. Source: ©Cartoon Resource.

Glaringly painful is the paradox of U.S. employers having to navigate the country's talent shortage with 7.5 million Americans unemployed as of March 2017, according to a U.S. Bureau of Labor Statistics report.[10] This, in light of millions more Americans working part-time jobs because they're unable to find full-time positions, or who have altogether given up looking for work. How can visionary business leaders work with education planners to train people with necessary job skills, to narrow the gap? Also important is for workers to realize the need for "learnability," the process to continue learning and adapting to remain hired over the long term.

Furthermore, CareerBuilder's 2016–2017 poll on the ever-widening skills gap conducted with over 10,000 respondents (with 4,771 employers and 6,626 employees) found almost 60 percent employers had job vacancies open for at least 12 weeks and longer. It costs a firm's human resources an average $800,000 annually for repeated job ads on vacancies and related expenses. In addition, this survey finds job vacancies increase for larger companies[11]:

- 1–50 employees: 49 percent
- 51–250 employees: 74 percent
- 251–500 employees: 72 percent
- 501+ employees: 71 percent

As revealing were responses from workers themselves. In March 2016, Harris Poll's survey for CareerBuilder found one in five employees (20 percent) said their skills were not current. Fifty-seven percent wanted to learn new skillsets to land better-paying and more fulfilling jobs. However, half said they could not afford to.

Forward wind to January 2018: what is the state of skills gaps two years later? Adecco, another staffing agency, in its survey of over 500 U.S. senior executives, found:

- 92 percent of business leaders say workers are not as skilled as they'd like them to be
- 44 percent think workers lack soft skills such as communication, creativity, critical thinking, and collaboration
- 64 percent think a lack of skilled workers will result in fewer U.S. business investments
- 59 percent blame this country's education system for gaps in workforce skills[12]

Skills in Demand

What are skills currently in demand by employers? CareerBuilder reported the most vacancies in 2016 were for heavy and tractor-trailer truck drivers, financial managers, sales managers, marketing managers, industrial engineers, web developers, demonstrators and product promoters, human resource managers, information security analysts, and general internists.[13]

In a similar vein, the UK's ManpowerGroup 2016/2017 survey found for the fourth consecutive year that skills shortfalls are most dire in the trades—such as electricians, carpenters, welders, bricklayers, and plumbers. The second category was for truck and heavy equipment drivers, with third most in demand skills for engineers (mechanical, electrical, and civil). Fourth were sales representatives (including executives and retail salespersons), with fifth most in demand being senior management executives. Sixth most needed professionals were doctors and non-nursing healthcare professionals, with office support staff coming in at seventh. Technicians (production, operations, maintenance) came in at eighth. Hospitality (restaurant and hotel) skills were needed at ninth, and nurses rounding off the top ten most in demand job skills in the UK.[14]

Barriers attracting top talent cited by employers include: the lack of available candidates (37 percent), candidates who lack necessary experience (17 percent), lacking hard skills such as technical competencies (16 percent), and lacking soft skills (9 percent). Twelve percent who were offered positions turned them down because candidates were looking for more pay.[15]

ManpowerGroup reported 40 percent of global managers express an urgent talent shortage. Increasingly, employers are training and reskilling existing employees to fill their open positions, increasing from one in five employers in 2006 to over half in 2016.[16]

Closing the Skills Gap

How can industries, education, and individuals work together to narrow the skills gap? According to economist Andrew Weaver in his *MIT Technology Review* (September 1, 2017) opinion piece,[17] the solution is simple. Weaver posits it is a matter for both sides, demand (employers) and supply (employees) to meet at common ground, to assess and implement solutions that are practical for both sides. For instance, from the business or demand side to look ahead and clarify needs assessments perhaps 10–15 years out, followed by project emerging and various evolving needs to be filled—to create education programs and practical training strategies to meet those needs.

Top corporations know they must continuously reskill and retrain employees to keep up with constantly evolving demands of the ever-changing marketplace. While the recipe for growing a skilled workforce may sound simple, practical implementation takes longer to effect over the course of more years ahead. Hence the need to start planning early and in advance, by anticipating changes to marketplace forces. These demands lay the foundation for common sense preplanning for preemployment training and boot camps. Typical needs scenarios are actually simple, as they perpetually call for industries to produce and market user-friendly products and services that are cost-effective to manufacture while being affordable to end-users.

To mitigate, even possibly reverse, this country's declining labor force participation, a Bloomberg opinion piece urges policy-makers, businesses, and educators to cocreate practical skills-training programs such as apprenticeships, cross-training, and retraining veterans to improve productivity. Improving worker skills offers upward mobility with higher-paying jobs. Closing the skills gap means recognizing the need to educate and train those without college degrees, too.[18]

Corroborating this call to think of new ways to educate and train workers without college degrees, the state of California is proposing an innovative idea to educate 2.5 million working adults—with online community college courses adapted for working students to take courses whenever they can, toward graduating with a degree. Students would not have to enroll at a physical location to follow the college's regular calendar year courses. Proposed by Eloy Ortiz Oakley, Chancellor of California Community Colleges, his vision seeks to narrow the income divide tied to education attainment.[19]

A study by IBM found 84 percent of top performing businesses provided employees with the relevant training they needed—compared to only 16 percent for employees with poorer performing companies. The reason being, when workers are continuously reskilled with ongoing new training to perform optimally, companies save an average $70,000 each year, while also enhancing productivity by 10 percent. These are all good reasons for businesses to implement job skilling and upskilling programs by employers and HR.[20]

"I am doing some retraining."

Figure 6.3. Source: ©Cartoon Resource.

Practical Skills Strategies to Implement

SHRM's 2016 survey found more than half of job applicants lacked basic skills, with 84 percent lacking applied skills. The lack of basic job and related applied skills is a huge factor contributing to talent shortages, resulting in disproportionately high job vacancies. "HR professionals from all industries report a highly competitive market for talent, with recruiting difficulty reaching levels not seen in years," said Jen Schramm, manager of SHRM's workforce trends and forecasting program. The highest levels of recruiting challenges were in health and social services, and manufacturing, with 46 percent saying it was hardest to recruit higher-level skilled medical positions. For smaller organizations with up to 99 employees, the difficulty was finding managers/project managers and skilled tradespeople.[21]

Thirty percent of respondents (out of 2,613 interviewed) lacked basic skills such as writing in English (grammar, punctuation, spelling) and computer skills (using a mouse, keyboarding, filing folders). Inadequate spoken English (18 percent), English reading comprehension (17 percent), math (14 percent), Spanish (8 percent), and science (6 percent) rounded off the litany of basic workforce skills that need to be addressed, for workers to be trained for a productive workforce.

SHRM found the lack of applied skills from 2,741 respondents interviewed were:

- critical thinking and problem-solving (45 percent)
- professionalism and work ethic, e.g., being punctual (43 percent)
- leadership (35 percent)
- written communications (29 percent)
- teamwork and collaboration (28 percent)
- oral communications (26 percent)
- application of information and communications technology (18 percent)
- lifelong learning and self-direction (16 percent), diversity (15 percent)
- creativity/innovation (14 percent)
- ethics/social responsibility (12 percent)[22]

HR professionals in this 2016 study say "new skills" required today are a mix of technical and applied skills. New skills call for a combination of soft skills such as communication, problem-solving, and teamwork (45 percent); followed by computer/web/IT proficiencies (39 percent); and management, project management, and training skills (39 percent). Technical skills (37 percent), plus business/HR/leadership skills (32 percent) are important for a robust workplace in keeping up with technological innovations. An emerging trend saw 30 percent full-timers sought new certifications, especially for those in larger businesses.[23]

Training new and current employees presents its own set of challenges to HR managers. It benefits employers to train and retrain current employees who can more quickly take on roles that are company specific, with the understanding it is harder for outside applicants to get up to speed. Yet, one-third surveyed reported their firms had no budget to train employees. Eleven percent reported training budgets were reduced in the past year. This apparent disconnect between HR and business owners needs to be addressed, SHRM noted. On middle ground, SHRM found 50 percent of training budgets were unchanged from the previous year. On the bright side, 39 percent of HR recruiters reported their budgets increased over the past year.

One important takeaway from SHRM's 2016 survey is for HR managers to better communicate to their employers the importance of job training and reskilling to address talent shortfalls. Rather than groaning about the skills gap and skill mismatches, it is more profitable to work proactively toward matching education and training needs with practical on-the-job mentoring and coaching with experienced employees.[24]

The private sector has the financial and human capital capabilities, plus the social responsibility, to close economics and skills gaps, according to a *Harvard Business Review* January 2017 article. Investors need to realign worker well-being with their money-making production interests. In fact, the research shows corporations have the money and the people to achieve more than governments. For example, the world's 500 largest corporations paid over $700 billion in taxes, revenues from their products and services raked in over $22 trillion, and they controlled assets valued at over $100 trillion.[25]

Takeaways

Meeting talent shortfalls and mitigating skills gaps can be guided by common sense analysis and practical planning from leaders working together for the good of the community, according to economists Andrew Weaver and Rob Kaplan. Education systems need to rethink curricula to include job-related instruction and skillsets, noted Pew Research Center. More recently, California's groundbreaking proposal provides online community college coursework for workers without degrees to pursue degrees and other credentials while working. Private corporations have the resources and social responsibility to give back to the public with related workforce training programs, higher wages, and other worker benefits—entrepreneurs, employers, and employees can stop waiting for the government to close the skills gap, noted Harvard Business School professor George Serafeim and coauthor John Streur.

Innovative ideas need commitment and dedication to see them through to fruition, by everyone. While mistakes are inevitable in working with unknowns, groundbreaking and creative experiences are also valuable for the learning insights they bestow. Most of all, we live in an age where lifelong learning, with the excitement of new discoveries, propels us towards anticipating and achieving ongoing revelations for industrial progress. Some trends are worth noting.

Forecasting specific emerging work trends. For example, AT&T, after informing 100,000 workers their jobs would be redundant in ten years, invested over $1 billion to retrain and upskill workers with a "Workplace 2020" initiative. Based on research to meet their projected consumer needs, AT&T is gearing up to be more agile and "on-demand" for customers. This strategy involves removing unnecessary traditional platforms in favor of higher-performing workspaces that are leaner, greener, and more supportive, enabling employees to collaborate easily.[26]

Collaborating on all levels to fill job vacancies. All sides need to recognize the challenge to honestly assess what programs are needed to benefit their communities. If marketing specialists know to market strategically to niche communities, why can't planning to fill unfilled jobs take a page to research and develop job-related instruction and job skilling needs unique to regional labor markets? And in the process, harness in-house resources such as having older experienced employees mentor and coach newer, younger generations adjust to the new firm?

Creating a company culture of creativity and agility. Progressive companies are ahead of the curve from *anticipating* consumer demands, while at the same time being aware of the need to be agile to adapt at the drop of a pin. Constantly *changing* marketplace forces will deal unexpected hands in various unknown ways; people and firms need to be nimble to meet headlong dynamic changes in this digital age of the Fourth Industrial Revolution.

Individual preparation. People must ask how they can best prepare for their own career advancement to plan ahead for practical and relevant education and job moves. As Pew Research Center found, 72 percent of individuals surveyed said it was their personal responsibility to obtain the necessary education and training themselves.[27] An individual's job search process is similar to AT&T revisiting its vision, to continuously analyze and fine-tune its mission to serve customers in new and improved ways, to stay vibrant and relevant, in any marketplace situation.

Likewise, for jobseekers to be on top of anticipating workplace requirements in sync with their career interests to continue doing what they love to do, while sharpening their chops learning job-related skills to offset as much career confusion as possible. Time spent researching your moves is time well spent. "If we knew what it was we were doing, it would not be called research, would it?" asked Albert Einstein.

In the course of my career, I've learned it pays to be always looking and planning my next move. It does not pay to be complacent, however financially secure the position is. People, firms, and work teams come and go, due to market forces (not on a person's aptitude or competencies). I've learned to look for transition signals, watch trends, plan next steps, and explore my interests such as business, education, and public speaking.

Career & Skill Planning Tips

My doctoral studies provided me with opportunities to teach while working. While working at Cisco, I taught BA-level business and women's studies classes, plus MBA courses, for Bay Area colleges on nights and weekends. Students were adults who worked in the day and pursued their degrees at night.

However, many lacked key business skills vital for today's workplace, such as communication and presentation skills, and teamwork collaboration. Other than basic computer skills, they were uncomfortable using technology at work. Most had experienced traditional pedagogy with one-way lectures, textbook reading, and written exams. I felt this arcane approach to learning was irrelevant for today's dynamic workplaces.

I approached my teaching with: group project assignments, class presentations using multimedia, group reading assignments of top business bestseller books with classroom discussions, exposure to a wide range of guest speakers from a variety of industries and jobs, discussions on current events and business news, and research projects on work and career options.

I invited students to tour Cisco's manufacturing plant. They were always thrilled when Randy Pond (then VP of manufacturing, now Cisco board member) dropped in with pizza to answer questions about tech manufacturing careers.

- Be purposeful about your education goals. Focus on how you'll use your degree or classes for work and career growth. Pick courses wisely; have a useful career degree, not just a degree. Ask: is a public speaking elective more useful than one in history?
- Adult learners come out ahead when combining course assignments with job-related projects. This is more meaningful to you and your management team at work.
- Take as many classes as your firm offers to pay, to build up skills needed; for example, finance, technology, operations.
- Full-time students: take core courses in first and second years. Research internships for first-year summer work. Save junior and senior years for electives, terms aboard, fine-tuning major.

- Use the classroom to fill in learning gaps. This is a safe place to practice, learn from others, and share your unique skills. Uncomfortable with presentations? This is the place to do it. If you don't understand technology, you're surrounded by people who do. Not a strong writer? Treat assignments as exercises to hone your writing skills, and work with the school's writing center.
- As an educator, I feel our role is to help students understand the world we live in, how they fit in, and learn to drive the future managing their careers. My guest speakers explained their jobs; education, skills, and experiences required to love doing what they do; how they planned their careers; and advice for adult learners. This is important for faculty to do.
- Its important for students to use work-related technology in assignments, be it multimedia for presentations, Excel for financial discussions, or Power Point for presentations. Technology is a useful language to learn; you become fluent using it.
- Learn two technologies related to your job or major. For example, if in manufacturing, learn about 3-D printing and robotics. Understand current and future landscapes to keep up, and to stay ahead.

Notes

1. Dan Schawbel, "10 Workplace Trends You'll See in 2018," *Forbes*, November 1, 2017, https://www.forbes.com/sites/danschawbel/2017/11/01/10-workplace-trends-youll-see-in-2018/#1c11177c4bf2.
2. Pew Research Center, "The State of American Jobs," October 6, 2016, www.pewsocial trends.org/2016/10/06/the-state-of-american-jobs/.
3. Ibid.
4. Ibid.
5. "Average Cost-per-Hire for Companies is $4,129, SHRM Survey Finds," August 3, 2016, https://www.shrm.org/about-shrm/press-room/press-releases/Pages/Human-Capital-Benchmarking-Report.aspx.
6. Sophie Quinton, "Why the 'Skills Gap' Doesn't Explain Slow Hiring," Pew Charitable Trusts, November 14, 2016, http://www.pewtrusts.org/en/research-and-analysis/blogs/stateline/2016/11/14/why-the-skills-gap-doesnt-explain-slow-hiring.
7. Ibid.
8. Ibid.
9. CareerBuilder, April 13, 2017, http://press.careerbuilder.com/2017-04-13-The-Skills-Gap-is-Costing-Companies-Nearly-1-Million-Annually-According-to-New-Career Builder-Survey.
10. Ibid.
11. Ibid.
12. https://www.adeccousa.com/employers/resources/skills-gap-in-the-american-workforce/.
13. CareerBuilder, April 13, 2017, http://press.careerbuilder.com/2017-04-13-The-Skills-Gap-is-Costing-Companies-Nearly-1-Million-Annually-According-to-New-Career Builder-Survey.

14. ManpowerGroup Infographic, http://www.manpowergroup.co.uk/wp-content/uploads/2016/10/2016_TSS_Infographic_UnitedKingdom.pdf.
15. Ibid.
16. "2016–2017 Talent Shortage," ManpowerGroup, n.d., 2016.
17. Andrew Weaver, "The Myth of the Skills Gap," MIT *Technology Review*, September 1, 2017, 76–79.
18. Rob Kaplan, "America Has to Close the Workforce Skills Gap," Bloomberg.com, April 12, 2017, https://www.bloomberg.com/view/articles/2017-04-12/america-has-to-close-the-workforce-skills-gap.
19. Claudio Sanchez, "Reinventing Community College to Reach Millions of Workers—Online," NPR.org, March 9, 2018, https://www.npr.org/sections/ed/2018/03/09/589113650/reinventing-community-college-to-reach-millions-of-workers-online.
20. Ibid.
21. "The New Talent Landscape Recruiting Difficulty and Skills Shortages," SHRM, 2016. "SHRM Survey: Employers Face Increased Challenges in Recruiting, Hiring Qualified Job Applicants." June 21, 2016, https://www.shrm.org/about-shrm/press-room/press-releases/pages/2016-recruiting-skills-gap-survey.aspx.
22. "The New Talent Landscape Recruiting Difficulty and Skills Shortages," SHRM, 2016.
23. Ibid.
24. Ibid.
25. John Streur & George Serafeim, "Stop Waiting for Governments to Close the Skills Gap," *Harvard Business Review*, January 11, 2017, https://hbr.org/2017/01/stop-waiting-for-governments-to-close-the-skills-gap.
26. https://www.att.jobs/workplace-2020.
27. Pew Research Center, "The State of American Jobs," October 6, 2016, www.pewsocialtrends.org/2016/10/06/the-state-of-american-jobs/.

· 7 ·

HIGHER EDUCATION PREPARES STUDENTS FOR JOBS, CAREERS, AND LIFE

This chapter discusses the purpose of America's higher education, as it evolves to meet the country's changing socioeconomic, business, and industrial needs. A significant shift today sees education moving away from one-stop schooling and expanding into lifelong learning. Continued training motivates individuals to strive to excel at work while also being fulfilled with healthy work–life balance. A second major trend is the changing role college career centers play in connecting and guiding students toward good-fit careers. A third notable trend is how corporations and educational institutions cocreate win–win instructional partnerships. The rationale? Industries need a pipeline of employable graduates who are knowledgeable about what and how working in various firms and industries entails. Students in turn are excited to explore career opportunities with the potential for full-time employment upon graduation.

College graduates trained to apply technology across industries are valued for their contributions to sustain America's robust economy. These efforts result in stimulating an educated, skilled, and vibrant workforce. I participated in an education–employer partnership strategy when I worked for Apple Computer, utilized Cisco's tuition reimbursement benefit, and ultimately earned my doctorate in business administration. This form of education–employer partnership is even more critical today, to buttress projected talent shortfalls and skills gaps as discussed in Chapter 6.

However, while our role as educators in higher education has not changed, various platforms for instruction have (e.g., online coursework, with more later in this chapter). We continue producing the pipeline of future talent to contribute in meaningful ways in the world they live. This means our students need proficient training to be competent fielding an array of roles they take on upon graduation. From creating successful and responsible businesses, to mentally and professionally prepared to work in organizations in a world we do not often understand. A world environment that's forcefully impacted by megatrends and the global forces of change—with purposeful higher education facilitating connections to help students interpret and develop their own meaningful destinies in the workforce. Students need to understand the diverse nature of our world and its myriad ecosystems, in getting along and collaborating with teamwork, and recognizing the unique role each person plays in their own way.

> I watched my sister go to college and graduate magna cum laude—but without landing a job in her profession due to the recession. She has huge loans and works multiple jobs trying to pay rent and pay off her debts. I'm not sure if this is what I want to do.
> —High School Senior

What Is the Purpose of Education?

The purpose of education in the First and Second Industrial Revolutions was vastly different from the Third and Fourth Industrial Revolutions. The latter two industrial revolutions have accelerated the pace of life and learning in under fifty years—while the former two revolutions took two hundred years to evolve. Yet, similar aspirations survive for education to thrive with fundamental functions teaching students to think and reflect purposefully. In 1930, America's longest-serving First Lady Eleanor Roosevelt (1933–1945) asked, "What is the purpose of education? This question agitates scholars, teachers, statesmen, every group, in fact, of thoughtful men and women."[1]

Historically, education in America has evolved to meet society's changing needs. For example, youth were initially taught religious studies, which later morphed into preparing them for responsible citizenship to live in a democracy. Education then shifted to assimilating immigrants into mainstream society, followed by training workers for the Second Industrial Revolution when the country began large-scale manufacturing and industrial production.[2]

In today's Fourth Industrial Revolution, Pew Research Center found six out of ten adult Americans in 2016 say K–12 public schools are responsible for teaching the workforce education and job skills essential for career success. Republicans (58 percent) say colleges should teach students job skills. Democrats split, 42 percent saying college should help the individual grow personally and intellectually, with 43 percent say college studies should teach specific skills.[3]

Fundamentally, "Education should prepare young people for life, work *and* citizenship. Knowledge of the natural and engineered environments and how people live in the world is critical to all three purposes of education. Critical thinking, creativity, interpersonal skills and a sense of social responsibility all influence success in life, work and citizenship," exhorts Arthur H. Camins in a *Washington Post* article dated February 12, 2015.[4]

The intrinsic value of a public higher education serves students with a civic-minded liberal education to support them both in life and in career, urges Bethany Zecher Sutton of the American Association of Colleges and Universities. "Critical thinking, problem solving, working in diverse teams, ethical reasoning, communicating—these make both good employees and good citizens," Sutton says. While it is understandable many parents look upon paying for a college education as an investment for their children's future employment, returns on investments would be even more pragmatic when parents "liberate mindsets" to also see education as contributing back to the civic good of all communities.[5]

I graduated with a psychology degree; that was what women did in my generation. I realized in my sophomore year that I did not want to become a psychologist or to teach. The degree helped me develop listening skills and observe behavior, but not useful for securing a job or establishing a career. I went back to school at night for an MBA and eventually more advanced degrees to keep on being employable.

—Procurement Manager

In 2015, Wisconsin Governor Scott Walker deleted two of the state's founding values of truth and service from the University of Wisconsin's mission statement, while proposing slashing $300 million off its annual budget (the university was founded in 1848, the same year Wisconsin became a state). Gov. Walker asserted the purpose of higher education was "to meet the state's workforce needs." He had to backtrack in the face of student and citizen protests.[6] Ultimately, the purpose of education is to develop skills that students can use to reflect and evaluate information intelligently, for outcomes to benefit them and the common good.

Figure 7.1. Source: ©Cartoon Resource.

Today, with the accelerating pace of technological innovations shaking up the workplace emphasizing digital savviness, the role of lifelong higher education has become even more central to employers and employees to keep a robust economy humming. Especially in light of an aging boomer workforce, who, as we have seen, is currently the largest employed age demographic. The majority of America's workforce needs to keep up to speed with digital enhancements developed and introduced at a much faster pace than before. The caveat from Georgetown University Center for Education and the Workforce in a 2010 report pointed out a projected shortfall of three million college graduates plus at least 4.7 million new workers with postsecondary certifications.[7]

> I graduated with a degree in history. I was on the college baseball team and had to balance college with sports. I liked history. A history degree is useful if you plan to go into politics or teach. Once I started working, I went back to school for technology classes and my MBA at night and weekends, so I could start my own firm.
>
> —Business Owner

Workers in their mid-thirties and over are reluctant to leave current jobs to enroll in school again (compared to the majority of campus populations noticeably in their twenties). Enter alternative instructional modes such as massive open online courses, aka MOOCs. MOOCs are the answer to corporate America's urgent needs to reskill and upskill workforces.

MOOCs Move Along Lifelong Learning

MOOCs offer convenient certifications for adult learners seeking to acquire new work credentials. As a versatile instruction platform, MOOCs offer flexibility to an individual's timeline to learn at their own pace. About one-third of adult learners seeking later-life education are aged 30–54 juggling learning, working, and living with young families—all of which might pose seemingly insurmountable challenges—but for MOOCs.[8]

It's inevitable for workers to constantly upskill with lifelong learning now firmly entrenched in the workplace for professional advancement. Otherwise, people become redundant with outdated skills, left behind, and, worse, unemployable. Thanks to automation and technology, the shelf life of skills has been immeasurably shortened, reports CareerBuilder CEO Matt Ferguson, and the reason for massive increases to reskill and upskill.[9]

> I graduated with a degree in philosophy. I think it was a very good degree to help me think more abstractly and still useful today. However, when I joined a high tech firm I had to increase my skills, learn new technologies to keep current, and to stay employed. Lifelong learning is a must today—no matter what job you pursue!
>
> —Marketing Manager

Universities are typically involved in developing course content for MOOCs, reports the *Economist*. Content is by design short and direct; for example, broken into segments of not more than six minutes for videos, and one course taking about one month to complete. Students work on completing a set number of courses for each module, with a number of successfully completed modules determining certification. There are various MOOC platforms.[10]

Udacity (udacity.com) offers certification it calls "nanodegrees." Students can receive instruction to build self-driving autonomous cars with instructors from BMW and Mercedes-Benz engineers. A website blurb touts, "Researchers estimate driverless cars will save 10 million lives per decade!" Various MOOCs offer different training platforms for certification and professional licensing. In addition, Udacity offers courses in robotics software, virtual reality, mobile Web, artificial intelligence, and robotics software engineering, among the gamut of data analytics and digital technologies. Emphasizing the need for lifelong learning, Udacity's 2018 Intersect Conference is to "Celebrate Lifelong Learning."[11]

Nvidia (nvidia.com), creator of the graphics processing unit or GPU that processes interactive images for gaming and other applications including reading texts on your devices (such as right now, if you're reading this on your Kindle) from computers to smartphones, is another MOOC instructional leader. Coursera (coursera.com) offers online content developed by university and IT specialists. Companies can integrate Coursera courses into their own instruction portals.[12] On its website, Coursera offers a six-course certification course developed by Google for entry-level IT support work valid for employment at Google, Walmart, Sprint, Infosys, and other corporations. Today, many IT positions are filled remotely; workers do not have to relocate, presenting yet another sweet spot for later-life students with family commitments—and signaling more breakthroughs for career trends that are people-friendly and convenient for lifelong learners.

Projecting future probability with 99.9 percent accuracy is possible nowadays, using mathematical algorithms and deep learning with machines (as

"How can we get 'retrained'? We never got trained."

Figure 7.2. Source: ©Cartoon Resource.

sixteen-year-old Brittany Wenger's breast cancer diagnosis app[13] showed). Data science reflects the emerging importance of data analytics as a scientific course of study, with high employment rates for graduates in all sectors of the world economy. Visionary leaders are able to look ahead and project education and training needs that are currently nonexistent—yet will be urgently needed all too soon.

What determines future projections for industry planners? How are MOOC courses developed as effective alternative instruction platforms for all stripes of learners, younger to older? As discussed in Chapter 4, mathematical algorithms are repeatedly engaged in deep learning using machine neural networks that perform similar to how the human mind functions. From repeated mining (aka deep learning) of data sets, seemingly inchoate and disparate information bits are mined down to the smallest details, for data-driven predictions on business planning, people, and every imaginable idea to innovate and improve on.[14] Projected trends assist in developing related courses, with relevant MOOC content expertly developed by educators, specialists, and professionals to meet professional and industrial needs.

I went to a sports, and some would say, party college. I had a great time and got a lot out of my system. I met my husband there, and we have two kids. I did not think college was a place to look for a job—but a place to spread your wings, meet people, socialize, and grow up. I am now a freelance contractor for various firms. I don't have a career, but I usually have jobs.

—Freelance Recruiter

Dell Technologies' 2017 report on *The Next Era of Human-Machine Partnerships* conducted by the Institute for the Future with twenty technology, academic, and business experts from around the world highlighted some futuristic trends such as:

- By 2030, every organization will become technological; businesses need to start future-proofing their infrastructure and workforce
- Workforce needs will chase people, where data-driven matchmaking will connect talent from around the world
- People "learn in the moment" from having to create new industries and new skills using, for example, augmented reality and virtual reality
- About 85 percent of jobs in 2030 have yet to be invented[15]

Future-proofing business survival is a huge challenge for every firm. This study found nearly one in two businesses believed they might possibly be obsolete in the next 3–5 years. Already, 52 percent of senior leaders have experienced business disruptions owing to digital advances.[16] Fortunately, one method saving industry skills from obsolescence is harnessing MOOCs to meet training needs, to mitigate the crush for continued reskilling affecting lifelong learners and employers.

Growth of College Career Centers

How do employers perceive college graduates are career ready and competent new employees? According to the National Association of Colleges and Employers (NACE), it depends. NACE identified eight areas of competencies for career readiness in college graduates. Employers considered graduates 65.8 percent competent in digital technology, while 59.9 percent students considered themselves competent. However, in seven competencies, employers perceived skills gaps in students, in comparison to higher scores students gave themselves.[17]

The greatest disparity surfaced in the area of professionalism and work ethics—where students saw themselves at 90 percent proficient, although less than half the employers agreed. Similarly, students graded themselves higher than employers did regarding oral and written communications and leadership capabilities. More students (85 percent) saw themselves proficient in teamwork, with employers agreeing at 75 percent.[18]

> I've graduates coming into the workforce totally clueless on how to communicate, contribute to meetings, present ideas, act appropriately at work. They have no sense of responsibility, no commitment; what it is like to work, and to manage a career. It's like they're still at a frat party. Education needs to prepare students for work.
>
> —HR Director

Before snagging a job that may turn out to be less of a good fit for them and their employers, students need to research as extensively as possible available job openings; and how they could possibly fit in professionally and personally into the work environment. College career centers offer support services to guide students, to explore and figure out good-fit options in finding jobs or graduate school programs. NACE urges students to work with career centers for employment prospects, while also calling for strong leadership to guide career centers.[19]

Yet, an *Atlantic* article notes many students do not prevail upon career centers. Moreover, 34 percent students lack confidence to participate in the job marketplace, and 36 percent in the workplace. Only 53 percent believed their majors would lead them to good jobs. Worse, only 20 percent students reached out to career centers. The article explains white students traditionally prevail on family connections for jobs, thus not contacting career centers. Minority and older students use career centers more, and are often their first encounters with career counseling.[20]

Career centers are getting relevant makeovers to meet current labor market demands. According to studies by Georgetown University Center for Education and the Workforce and Hanover Research, career centers are more proficient today connecting students with career pathways. Career centers analyze skills gaps needs of potential employers with job placements for graduates; counsel individuals on career pathways; organize "experiential education" with internships, employer-led workshops, and career fairs; and work more in line with education projections for workforce expansion to meet growing business demands for graduates to hire. All are good reasons for students to utilize career centers.[21]

I graduated with a master's in education and became an elementary school teacher. I burnt out after five years, teaching and coaching student sports teams to make ends meet. I talked to many colleagues to learn about what kinds of careers might make sense for me. I wanted to work 9 to 5. I have an interest in science, and of course kids. After lots of discussions, I decided to go back to school to be a pharmacist. It is hard work, and I hope this second career pays off.

—Pharmacist

Students need to think early on how to transition from education to vocation. To get you thinking about your career development, counselors ask questions such as: What are your interests, hobbies, and strengths? Why are you in this field of study? Do you see yourself in this field long term? Career centers coach students on resume writing, job interviews, and other tips.

A starter list on career centers includes:

- Stanford BEAM, https://beam.stanford.edu/
- Case Western Reserve, https://students.case.edu/career/
- Miami Dade College, http://www.mdc.edu/north/careercenter/
- Dalhousie University, Canada
- https://www.dal.ca/campus_life/career-and-leadership/job-resources-services.html
- Ben Franklin Career Center, http://benfranklinctc.weebly.com/

My parents wanted me to attend college. I was very shy. I went to a state school, and hated it. I was overwhelmed. I dropped out and moved home. I was too immature to handle being away from home. I worked at a neighbor's dental office until the dentist retired. I could not find a job without a degree, so I went back to night and weekend school to finish the degree. I did, and eventually got a job in government as an assistant.

—Administrative Assistant, Washington DC

Education–Employer Partnerships

Education–employer partnerships are creative solutions to fill skills gaps for industries, while providing employment for students transitioning into the workplace upon graduation. Businesses assess hiring needs and collaborate with educators and school career centers to develop proficiencies in: (a) effective leadership, (b) learnability, to learn and adapt technical applications on the job, (c) situational awareness to serve professionally, and (d) job skills.[22]

Alarmed about the skills gap and its impact on America's economy, top CEOs convened the Business Roundtable (BusinessRoundtable.org) to spearhead innovative approaches to train a qualified workforce for corporate America. Its 2016 Talent Survey found three main skills gaps:

- Individuals lack basic skills; namely math, effective communication, reading technical manuals, teamwork, and problem solving
- Lack of specialized tradespeople for specific skilled jobs
- Lack of science, technology, engineering, and math skills (STEM) skilled workers[23]

Education and employers need to be more in sync. I interview a lot of graduates who come to the workplace unprepared for work. Imagine, a finance major did not know how to use Microsoft Excel spreadsheet, a business basic in the corporate world. Something has to change!

—Finance Manager

The private sector spends over $164 billion every year to educate and reskill workers to meet corporate needs—and is still falling behind. *How CEOs Are Helping Close America's Skills Gap* is a report of how top U.S. corporations tackle their talent shortages in creative ways. The main strategies employed are: (a) collaborating with educational organizations to sponsor job training programs, (b) apprenticeships, (c) tuition reimbursement, and (d) reskilling and upskilling opportunities for current employees. Business Roundtable corporations include: 3M, Aon, Best Buy, Boeing, Cisco, DOW, Eastman, Exxon, Harris, Huntington Ingalls, KPMG, Lockheed, Northrop, Qualcomm, SAP, SAS, Starbucks, Texas Instruments, Textron, and Visa.

Another major wrinkle CEOs grapple with is closing the gap with women and minorities, who are still underrepresented in corporate America and particularly in STEM occupations. In 1993, 23 percent of STEM workers were female; twenty years later, in 2013, women were 29 percent—still under two-thirds of STEM workers. Seventy percent CEOs found it problematic to hire a diverse workforce for computer and math, architecture, sales, business and finance, life and physical sciences, and the social sciences.[24]

I'm a librarian. My daughter clearly excels in math and science, which are out of my expertise. I try to find her role models in these fields with the help of neighbors and the career center at her college, so she can see other successful women in math and science. I don't want her to get off track with her goal to be a scientist. Even though it is out of my realm of expertise, I want to keep her on track.

—Librarian, California

Perhaps one way to close the skills gap more quickly is to educate potential workers at an earlier age. Oracle completed a $43 million charter high school, Design Tech High School (designtechhighschool.org) aka "d.tech" on its campus in December 2017. Open to residents of California, all 550 students pay no tuition. Students are free to follow their dreams with academic rigor and creative problem solving. However, they must first learn to empathize with humans before creating solutions for their problems. And while Oracle employees are available to mentor students, d.tech develops its own curricula, hires its own faculty and staff, with its own school board—all independent of Oracle.[25]

Toyota, W. M. Keck Foundation, and California State University at Dominguez Hills debuted four "fab labs" in September 2017, to bring mobile fabrication labs to high schools in Los Angeles County. These design labs

Figure 7.3. Source: ©Cartoon Resource.

on wheels teach digital fabrication and computer literacy skills; many high schools in the area lack such labs.[26]

> I went to a large state university, in a big city with many distractions—beaches, shopping, nightlife. I was not mature. I could not handle it. I spent more time off-campus rather than focus on schoolwork. I dropped out and moved home. Both my parents are scientists. My father insisted I finish my degree (with a technology major) in a very good, local, small, private, four-year college within driving distance from home. He hovered throughout the process to make sure I stayed on track. I am glad I did. I'm now employed in a very good job, with a top tech firm in a growing industry.
>
> —Project Manager, Silicon Valley

It pays students to check out numerous innovative employer–education partnerships such as IBM's design classes for non-designers at the University of Texas, Austin; students explore real-world problems IBM is actually working on.[27] UPS' tuition program, "Earn and Learn," pays part-timers $5,250 each year toward tuition and maxing out at $25,000. UPS staff start as part-timers, learning and earning their stripes in upskilling and becoming tomorrow's executives.[28] Over 140,000 Starbucks employees (full- and part-time) can tap into free full tuition for 49 online degree courses (at time of writing) offered in partnership with Arizona State University. Starbucks' College Achievement Plan does not require employees to stay upon graduation.[29]

These are only some samples of groundbreaking job programs for skilling and tuition reimbursement. Top U.S. corporations identify parameters of skilling and training programs they offer in the Business Roundtable's free online publication, *How CEOs Are Helping Close America's Skills Gap* mentioned earlier.[30] To reiterate, career centers are valuable resources, too.

Tracey Transition Tips

Journeying through life is an adventure—of career twists and turns. K–12, I went to an all-girl Catholic school where the nuns focused on math, science, computer skills, and women as leaders. I went on to a four-year liberal arts college. Many of my classmates did not attend college, yet secured good jobs with the high school degree. After graduating college, I worked in New York City in media/fashion industry sales. I had no plans to return to school.

I moved to Palo Alto, California and was unemployable because it was techie high ground. My media sales experience was not relevant for Bay Area jobs. I worked three jobs (retail, hospitality, temporary admin work). I eventually got into Apple Computer; and told a liberal arts degree was not the right kind, or enough education, for Silicon Valley. I pursued the MBA while working with Apple's tuition reimbursement program and took their technology classes.

I left Apple, went on to HP, then Cisco. I wanted to pursue the doctorate in business administration (DBA) to keep ahead of the curve. At Cisco, their tuition reimbursement program helped me achieve my goal, as I continued with technology classes they offered.

A colleague alerted me to a visiting scholar program at Stanford University's Media X program funded by Reuters, the global news agency. They were looking for people with doctorates, a technology background, and interested in solving problems for underserved communities using technology. I had done a lot of work to advocate for women in technology. I applied and was selected.

Working at Cisco as their Higher Education Practice Lead was a full-time job, so I became a part-time visiting scholar on weekends and nights. I was amazed at the people I met at Stanford. Sergey Brin, Google co-founder. Vint Cerf, Internet co-founder. Russ Altman, geneticist. John Hennessy, tenth president of Stanford. Daphne Koller and Andrew Ng, Cousera co-founders who are no longer there.

I teamed up with a medical doctor to explore delivering preventative health education for diabetes and hypertension using multimedia via the Internet. This project targeted illiterate, underserved rural communities in Mexico, mainly through the women. My colleague was based in Mexico, with our project administered through the university Tech De Monterrey (tec.mx/en). http://mediax.stanford.edu/page/tracey-wilen-daughenti

After I left Cisco, I continued as visiting scholar at Stanford through the Apollo Group. My research expanded to women in leadership, published into the book *Women Lead* (Peter Lang, 2013), and still well received. I left Apollo and started my own business as a speaker, author, and media contributor, and have enjoyed running it for over five years. Whether working in a firm or on my own, continuous learning has been a necessity.

- Lifelong learning is very important to remain relevant. Be purposeful about education choices, not necessarily a degree, but a skill, trade, certification, or whatever the job requires.
- Education is expensive and time-consuming. Align with firms offering tuition reimbursement and reskilling/training benefits, in combining work with education for a more meaningful experience.
- Career planning is important, more so than in the past. There are many more options and different requirements. Create your own outcomes, with continuous education as part of your career strategy.
- Everyone is dealt a hand (as in a poker game). It's up to you to find your aces, jokers, and wild cards. Play your own hand smartly—not someone else's.
- Access to education is readily available. Individuals need to research content, learn to keep on learning, to stay relevant and employable.
- An educator, my job is to connect students to realities and opportunities of the world they live in, to provide access and connections for them to succeed as skilled professionals.

Notes

1. Willona M. Sloan, "What is the Purpose of Education?" Association for Supervision and Curriculum Development, July 2012, http://www.ascd.org/publications/newsletters/education-update/jul12/vol54/num07/What-Is-the-Purpose-of-Education¢.aspx.
2. Ibid.
3. Kristen Bialik, "Most Americans Say K-12 Schools Have a Lot of Responsibility in Workforce Preparation," Pew Research Center, August 25, 2017, http://www.pewresearch.org/fact-tank/2017/08/25/most-americans-say-k-12-schools-have-a-lot-of-responsibility-in-workforce-preparation/.
4. Valerie Strauss, "What's the Purpose of Education in the 21st Century?" *Washington Post*, February 12, 2015, https://www.washingtonpost.com/news/answer-sheet/wp/2015/02/12/whats-the-purpose-of-education-in-the-21st-century/?utm_term=.dd684b5ca0b9.
5. Bethany Zecher Sutton, "Higher Education's Public Purpose," American Association of Colleges & Universities, June 20, 2016, https://www.aacu.org/leap/liberal-education-nation-blog/higher-educations-public-purpose.
6. Alice Miranda Ollstein, "Scott Walker Deletes the Values of Truth and Service from University Mission," February 6, 2015, https://thinkprogress.org/scott-walker-deletes-the-values-of-truth-and-service-from-university-mission-d107c62cbc16/.
7. Anthony P. Carnevale, Nicole Smith, & Jeff Strohl, "Help Wanted: Projections of Jobs and Education Requirements in Through 2018," Georgetown University Center on Education and the Workforce, June 10, 2010, https://cew.georgetown.edu/wp-content/uploads/2014/12/HelpWanted.ExecutiveSummary.pdf.
8. Special Report, "The Return of the MOOC," *Economist*, January 12, 2017, https://www.economist.com/news/special-report/21714173-alternative-providers-education-must-solve-problems-cost-and.
9. Matt Ferguson, "What Will It Take to Close the Skills Gap? Take an Educated Guess," June 2, 2017, http://www.clomedia.com/2017/06/02/will-take-close-skills-gap-take-educated-guess/.
10. Special Report, "The Return of the MOOC," *Economist*, January 12, 2017, https://www.economist.com/news/special-report/21714173-alternative-providers-education-must-solve-problems-cost-and.
11. https://blog.udacity.com/2018/02/celebrate-lifelong-learning-udacity-intersect-2018.html.
12. Ibid.
13. Chelsea Whyte, "Brittany Wenger, 17, Wins Google Science Fair with Revolutionary App to Diagnose Breast Cancer," July 25, 2012, www.isciencetimes.com/articles/3502/20120725/brittany-wenger-17-wins-google-science-fair.htm.
14. Michael Copeland, "What's the Difference Between Artificial Intelligence, Machine Learning, and Deep Learning?" Nvidia blog, July 29, 2016, https://blogs.nvidia.com/blog/2016/07/29/whats-difference-artificial-intelligence-machine-learning-deep-learning-ai/.
15. Dell Technologies, "Realizing 2030: Dell Technologies Research Explores the Next Era of Human-Machine Partnerships," *Cision PR Newswire*, July 12, 2017, https://www.prnewswire.com/news-releases/realizing-2030-dell-technologies-research-explores-the-next-era-of-human-machine-partnerships-300486894.html.

16. Ibid.
17. NACE Staff, "Are College Graduates Career Ready?," February 19, 2018, http://www.naceweb.org/career-readiness/competencies/are-college-graduates-career-ready/.
18. Ibid.
19. Emanuel Contomanolis, Christine Cruzvergara, Farouk Dey, & Trudy Steinfeld, "The Future of Career Services is Now," NACE, November 2, 2015, http://www.naceweb.org/career-development/trends-and-predictions/the-future-of-career-services-is-now/.
20. Lolade Fadulu, "Why Aren't College Students Using Career Services?" *The Atlantic*, January 20, 2018, https://www.theatlantic.com/education/archive/2018/01/why-arent-college-students-using-career-services/551051/.
21. Anthony P. Carnevale, Tanya I. Garcia, & Artem Gulish, "Career Pathways: Five Ways to Connect College and Careers," NACE, July 11, 2017, https://cew.georgetown.edu/cew-reports/careerpathways/. Hanover Research, "21st Century Recruiting and Placement Strategies," May 2014, http://www.hanoverresearch.com/media/21st-Century-Recruiting-and-Placement-Strategies.pdf.
22. Taryn Oesch, "Partnerships with Educational Institutions Help to Fill Skill Gaps and Create Confident Employees," *Training Industry*, December 6, 2017, https://trainingindustry.com/articles/workforce-development/partnerships-with-educational-institutions-help-to-fill-skill-gaps-and-create-confident-employees/.
23. Business Roundtable.org, "How CEOs are helping Close America's Skills Gap," June 2017, http://businessroundtable.org/sites/default/files/immigration_reports/2017.06.01%20BRT.Work%20in%20Progress.How%20CEOs%20Are%20Helping%20Close%20America's%20Ski....pdf.
24. Ibid.
25. Natasha Singer, "Now on Oracle's Campus, a $43 Million Public high School," December 3, 2017, https://www.nytimes.com/2017/12/03/technology/now-on-oracles-campus-a-43-million-public-high-school.html?module=ArrowsNav&contentCollection=Technology&action=keypress&region=FixedLeft&pgtype=article.
26. Toyota USA Newsroom, "Toyota and California State University, Dominguez Hills Dedicate Mobile Fabrication Laboratories to Bring STEM Learning to Schools in the Los Angeles Area," September 27, 2017, http://corporatenews.pressroom.toyota.com/releases/toyota+california+state+university+dominguez+hills+dedicate+mobile+fabrication+laboratories.htm.
27. Harry McCracken, "IBM Develops a Design Class for Non-Designers," *Fast Company*, October 26, 2017, https://www.fastcodesign.com/90147355/ibm-develops-a-design-class-for-non-designers.
28. https://www.jobs-ups.com/earn-and-learn.
29. "Starbucks and ASU Offer Four Years of College with Full Tuition Coverage," April 6, 2015, https://news.starbucks.com/news/starbucks-and-asu-expand-college-achievement-plan-full-tuition-coverage.
30. Business Roundtable.org, "How CEOs are helping Close America's Skills Gap," June 2017, http://businessroundtable.org/sites/default/files/immigration_reports/2017.06.01%20BRT.Work%20in%20Progress.How%20CEOs%20Are%20Helping%20Close%20America's%20Ski....pdf.

SECTION III

CAREER PLANNING—PREPARING FOR FUTURE JOBS AND CAREERS

· 8 ·

SHIFTING ORGANIZATIONS AND TALENT MANAGEMENT

This chapter explains today's shifting organizational structures and their impact on the career paths of employees—in turn affecting the organization's productivity and profitability throughout every cycle of its interconnected ecosystems. Firms *know* they need to be strategic and proactive with "always-on" learning strategies for employees, to retain them longer in helping them build satisfying careers, plus minimizing disruptions already brought on by digital advances and other unknown workplace disruptions. For example, Dell Technologies and the Institute for the Future project about 85 percent of jobs in 2030 are yet to be created.[1] CEOs and human resource (HR) managers face myriad challenges to incorporate accelerating digital innovations and related adoption challenges by employees—while also having to deal with expanding multigenerational workforces. We discuss how to work with and develop career successes for multigenerational workforces, and ideas for effective retention strategies.

My manager told me our company has a new employment philosophy. I should change jobs every 2–4 years, and to apply for internal openings. That it would be better for my career advancement. I joined with the intent of progressing up the ladder as a specialist. I had my career all mapped out. Now I am totally confused.

—Manager, Fortune 100 firm

Urgent Need for Talent Management and Development

What can a CEO or HR manager do, in light of careening technological changes affecting emerging human capital trends that are constantly in flux? Deloitte's report on *2017 Global Human Capital Trends*[2] finds such speedy changes already rewriting HR rules for this digital age. (Deloitte has been studying emerging human capital trends since 2012.) Surveying 10,447 business and HR leaders from 140 countries, Deloitte delineated ten major trends for 2017:

- Many companies are racing to replace structured hierarchy with agile (fast moving, flexible) teams, with "the organization of the future arriving now;" 88 percent rated it as very important or important.
- Career learning in real time is critical for employees to learn quickly, easily: 83 percent.
- Talent acquisition is the third most important challenge: 81 percent.
- Employee experience is important to understand, to better retain them longer with a company culture that engages employee productivity and for company profits: 79 percent.
- Performance management is no longer based on annual employee reviews, but replaced with instant feedback and mentoring to increase productivity and enhance culture: 78 percent.
- New leaders are more agile, diverse, younger, and thrive in rapidly changing workplace environments: 78 percent.
- HR becomes a leader in digital organizations, reporting directly to the CEO: 73 percent.
- Digital analytics help understand what drives employee performance: 71 percent.
- Diversity, inclusion, equity—with a new focus on accountability, fairness, and transparency—are still fraught with frustration as reflected in huge reality gaps: 69 percent.
- An augmented workforce today includes outside hires such as freelance contractors, temps, and gig economy workers while in-house employment is streamlined: 63 percent.

The Boston Consulting Group (BCG)'s 2017 report announces similar findings, in reiterating how demand for scarce top talent, talent management, and the need for talent development are reshaping hiring practices worldwide.

Firms are forced to continue investing resources for massive skills redevelopment—even as half of U.S. jobs will be automated by 2050—in seismic shifts fueled by the global access to information from an estimated 7.6 billion digital users who will own 11.6 billion devices by 2020. Galloping globalization in trade and information exchanges necessitate simplifying complex procedures (74 percent managers surveyed say complexity hurt performance outcomes). Agility is critical for executing improved outcomes, say 90 percent managers. For example, 66 percent of consumers in 60 countries are willing to pay more for eco-friendly goods, showing how quickly a new trend like the green movement is adopted as mainstream practice.[3]

Our increasing digital consumption in every sphere of personal and professional lifestyle interactions has led to the exponential explosion of big data and the science of data analytics in every arena. BCG estimates big data will unlock $1 trillion of business value by 2020. Thus, the implication for HR is the necessity to use and adapt big data for people analytics—to predict people affiliation and possible good fit in firms, team dynamics, and retention. Firms are finding they must adopt data analytics not just in HR but also in every department to seamlessly access data, plus enabling workers to collaborate in real time through online connections. Estimated daily data churns are 2.5 quintillion data bytes.[4]

Managers Matter for Employee Productivity

Who will facilitate employees to learn new skills and adapt training for best practices in HR? The research points to good managers. A 2017 LinkedIn study finds companies are upping spending for learning and development (L&D) by 27 percent. The reasons are to foremost develop managers and leaders; followed by assisting employees developing technical skills; training everyone in a cohesive way; and supporting employee career development.[5]

The top two priorities focus on improving manager coaching and communication skills. Noticeably, while both large and smaller companies emphasize L&D, the former highlights overall career development for employees. Smaller companies tilt toward developing technical skills in their employees.[6]

> I asked my manager if I could make a lateral move to increase my experience and skills. I was told to leave, get the experience somewhere else, and then come back in the new role. Is that confusing or what?
>
> —Director, Fortune 500 firm

Good bosses are doubtless critical for the overall health of the firm. Leaders and managers know how much of an impact they have on their workers—including matters of life-or-death. Stockholm's Stress Research Institute followed 3,100 men over ten years and found 60 percent were more susceptible to life-threatening cardiac arrests, especially for those who didn't respect their bosses. Three out of four employees said bad bosses were the worst and most stressful part of their jobs. Not surprisingly, organizations are half as productive because bad bosses kill productivity.[7]

In fact, Gallup's 2015 *State of the American Manager* report finds only 35 percent of managers actively engaged in their work. Managers with high talent (defined as naturally capable of excellence) were 54 percent more engaged, compared to 27 percent of managers with limited talent. Managers in the middle (with functioning or moderate talent) are also less engaged in the workplace.[8]

Developing new leadership is a priority for 86 percent of companies, with 85 percent of executives lacking confidence in their leaders. Surprisingly, 65 percent employees prefer new bosses to pay raises.[9]

Ninety-three percent of managers feel they need coaching to train employees. While management may be inclined to select individuals with stellar contributions and personalities to lead projects, studies find it is better to carefully promote and train those with leadership capabilities. In fact, many sharp prolific producers prefer not to become managers. The key is to train managers to be empathic coaches, coaxing and motivating productivity from employees for the overall healthy benefit of the firm. Effective managers communicate well and engage in honest and meaningful discourse with team members. Managers today give ongoing constructive feedback to show they care in cultivating positive relationships for happier employees. Given these skills, managers are expected to coach and empower their teams on to higher productivity levels, while minimizing spending energies in constant back-and-forth with team members.[10] All of which also enhance career development for everyone, to benefit employers and employees.

The role of the manager has changed. When I started working the manager told us what to do. Then it shifted to a working manager who had to be a working expert and also manage staff. Today a manager needs to be a leader, helping guide the organization's future. This means employees need to take responsibility for their own jobs and careers—and look to their manager as an advisor, not a parent. Our employees are confused. I'm not sure if anyone clearly explained the shift to them.

—Baby Boomer, Fortune 500 firm

Career Management Is Tops

A LinkedIn *Workplace Learning Report* spots the following trends for 2018, calling for urgent talent and career development. The first trend identifies the importance of training employees to acquire soft skills in the new workplace. Soft skills desired in four core areas are: leadership, communication, collaboration, and role-specific skills. Acquiring soft skills enhances an individual's confidence to execute job functions.[11]

The second essential is to spend time probing and identifying industry trends that are developing, to project job needs well in advance as accurately as possible, to avoid internal skill gaps. With the short shelf life of skillsets, the third trend calls for understanding the impact of technology on firms and using online learning courses as a major solution to reskilling employees.[12]

However, employees are not making time to learn new skills, which this study finds is the fourth challenge. (And double-edged, with 94 percent employees saying they would stay if the company invested in their careers— even as management wants them to stay on top with learning new skills.) Fifth, manager encouragement is crucial for employees to learn new skills; 56 percent would take a course if suggested by their manager.

> I applied to a job opening at my firm in hopes of finding a better fit for my skills. HR told me it was only for outside applicants and to withdraw my application. What kind of confused message is that?
>
> —Individual Contributor, Manufacturing firm

The LinkedIn report concludes with a World Economic Forum recommendation, "As the rate of skills change accelerates across both old and new roles in all industries, proactive and innovative skill-building and talent management is an urgent issue. What this requires is a talent development function that is rapidly becoming more strategic and has a seat at the table."[13] (HR increasingly reports directly to the CEO, as also noted by Deloitte in the previous reference.)

Employees are generally lifelong jobseekers, searching for good-fit occupations that bring them job satisfaction—and happiness. Zappos CEO Tony Hsieh's 2010 book *Delivering Happiness* published after he sold Zappos to Amazon in 2009 in a deal valued at $1.2 billion. Zappos' top priority focuses on developing a positive company culture, where personal and professional developments are valued—for happy employees to better serve customers.[14]

> I remember when a group of us single and working parents petitioned our CEO for flextime and job sharing. He flatly denied, stating these were non-productive part-time jobs. Confused and disappointed with his lack of life realities, we left the firm and found better jobs elsewhere.
>
> —Office Manager, Fortune 500 firm

At the time of writing, LinkedIn's analysis of the *Top Companies: Where the US Wants to Work Now 2018* spotlights fifty stellar companies. Data are culled from job-seeking LinkedIn U.S. members (146 million in the United States; total 546 million worldwide) who indicated interest in the company and engaged with employees, job demand, and employee retention. The top ten are[15]:

1. Amazon; the United States' second-largest private company employs over 566,000
2. Alphabet; parent company of Google, controls global search activities
3. Facebook; with 2 billion monthly users worldwide
4. Salesforce; cloud-based business software, with a 35 percent minority workforce
5. Tesla; engineers ship code without having to go through "eight layers of approval"
6. Apple; with over 500 Apple stores worldwide
7. Comcast NBCUniversal; hired over 36,000 new employees in 2017
8. The Walt Disney Co.; continues to "imagineer," now hiring data scientists
9. Oracle; enterprise software and hardware for over 430,000 businesses in 175 countries
10. Netflix; "spends heavily" on a dream team with ambitious, common goals

While the majority require college and advanced degrees, some encourage applicants with high school degrees to apply (e.g., Box), providing in-house training for their own unique needs.

> My dad was an engineer, always tinkering with technology and showing me how things worked. It was very inspiring, so I went into computer science. I think it is important for parents to share their interests with kids, for us to see what career options are out there.
>
> —Engineer, High Technology firm

In addition to stressful work environments, employees can carry personal burdens such as "midcareer crises." Research shows employee satisfaction bottoms out at the person's career midpoint. Many companies are unaware of this phenomenon, let alone develop strategies to address it, thus setting in motion huge losses of precious human capital, notes Josh Bersin, Deloitte's principal of human capital. When these workers leave, Bersin explains, "Losing the institutional knowledge, honed skill sets, and employee trust and cooperation that have been accrued by mid-career employees is costly—to the tune of 213 percent of an employee's salary in one year, in some cases."[16]

As challenges brew to reskill and continuously upskill employees to work more efficiently with ever-new digital technologies, it also means having to introduce newer, shifting organizational structures into the workplace to accommodate changing work processes. Workers and managers are scrambling to figure out how to work within traditional job hierarchies that are often less efficient in getting goods and services swiftly and cost-effectively to the marketplace. The critical need is to develop agile work teams for the new workplace as noted in studies cited previously. Agile teams score when they

"I've been re-calculating my career."

Figure 8.1. Source: ©Cartoon Resource.

ably react spontaneously and skillfully to unknowns brought on by shifting consumer market demands—where the only constant is change.

> I work in a traditional hierarchical firm that is trying to change its organization. I was totally bored in my job. HR created a new job track for more entrepreneurial employees to become "project managers." I look for a project to join or lead, inside the firm. Once the project ends, I look for a new opening, still within the firm, and negotiate my own salary based on my skills and experiences. It's like getting a new job every few years. I have met and worked with many executive senior leaders in the firm. Confusing at first, but I think it pays off later.
>
> —Project Manager, Healthcare firm

Shifting Organizations

Shifting, newer agile organizational structures are on collision course with silent and boomer generations, who expect to move up the employment ladder via traditional hierarchical avenues, such as dutifully showing up daily for facetime at work, reporting to a manager with yearly performance reviews, and gradually climbing up career ladders at work.

Enter generations Xers, Yers (or millennials), and Zers—born during the Third and Fourth Industrial Revolutions—natural-born techies who are perfect for disruptive companies. They prefer to work in agile project teams with the flexibility to laterally and literally move around (in fact, many are joined to the hip with their mobile desks) to work on team projects that appeal to them. Compounding this situation is the medley of multigenerational workers typically sprinkled throughout a firm.

How are organizational structures shifting? How are newer organizational structures affecting talent management and career development? How can business leaders gainfully employ a workforce of multigenerations within their shifting organizations?

Hierarchical Organizations

> I was hired on Friday. On Monday when I started, I had a new manager. By the end of the week, my department was reorganized. The following week we had a new leadership team. I feel like I'm bounced around not knowing where I will be next. I'm told to be engaged and productive. How can you do that when you don't know who or where you will be working for on any given day of the week? I am totally confused!
>
> —Marketing Manager, High Growth Firm

Historically, firms operated in hierarchical structured matrices of command and control, from top on down. Employees were assigned roles that were clearly defined. Managers were not leaders (although in the new workplace they are both), but corralled workers to perform according to company projects reflecting its vision and mission. There was a sense of departmental loyalty among workers in top-down organizations. Employees received annual reviews, moved up, and got promoted according to the previous year's performances—a yearly exercise that was traditionally undertaken, and expected, for career advancement in structured hierarchies.[17]

> I am a single parent. I need a stable, predictable job so I can be available for my kids. I'm confused. Am I penalized in my career because I have kids?
>
> —Finance Manager

Flat Organizations

However, the new workplace generally means working flat, in an organizational structure very different from a hierarchy. Flat organizations have become even more popular with digital age workers. Employees work and engage in teams, and across teams, sans middle managers to produce faster, newer iterations of products. Gaming producer Valve was boss-free in its early years (beginning in 1996). Compensation was determined by team members, and instead of promotions, people moved on to new projects, gaining more experience and increasing paychecks along the way (or voted out and let go). Valve's employees literally move around on mobile desks. Yet, older forms of flat organizations have been around where teams work productively without bosses, such as Gore-Tex founded in 1958 with over 10,000 employees.[18]

In the 1950s, coal miners in South Yorkshire, England, increased productivity when they worked in self-managed teams. Multi-skilled autonomous teams interchanged roles with minimal supervision, mining away 24 hours nonstop. Self-managed teams morphed into various forms; for example, in Japan they became quality circles with team efforts at continuous self-improvement. Volvo's plant in Kalmar, Sweden, reduced defects by 97 percent in 1987. General Mills increased productivity by 40 percent in mills with self-managed teams. In a way, self-managed teams or holacracies do resemble hierarchical control—but without interference from whimsical bosses.[19]

**"What we've done is make it dramatically easier
to navigate the corporate hierarchy."**

Figure 8.2. Source: ©Cartoon Resource.

Holacracy

Holacracy's three main characteristics are: (a) highly adaptable and agile teams that make up the firm's structure; (b) teams design their own designated products and govern themselves; (c) leadership is distributed among team roles that people play-work at, not individuals, with leadership constantly shifting as projects changed along with new roles defined each time, for each new project. The authors of a *Harvard Business Review* article caution though that holacracy is unsuitable for retail banking and defense contracting. How a firm adopts and adapts holacracy to meet their unique needs matters hugely, as in the case of online shoe retailer, Zappos.[20]

Many Zappos employees quit because roles were not well-defined before implementing halocracy for a corporation with over 1,500 employees. Employees were confused. Workers let on to the *New York Times* they didn't know how to work. For instance, Zappos payroll managers didn't know how to determine payroll with job titles gone. Others wanted to consult a boss before making important decisions.[21]

A study by professors Larissa Tiedens (Stanford University) and Emily Zitek (Cornell University) find people still prefer the traditional pecking order over flat organizations.[22] Workers say being flat is disorienting, reports Stanford professor Jeffrey Pfeffer. Hierarchical structures are more predictable and easier to figure out what people do and, as well, determine salaries. Hierarchies are practical and psychologically comforting. Most important, hierarchies have worked over time, and continue to do so, Pfeffer notes.[23]

Organizations' Transition to Agility

Yet, the organizational shift is inevitable, in tilting toward agility. Perhaps not in totality that's all out, flat out, for a flat organization at first, but a gradual adaptation to fit in distributed technologies to benefit an organization's

"We have finally achieved simplicity in our corporate organization."

Figure 8.3. Source: ©Cartoon Resource.

unique needs to meet growing demands for incorporating digital savviness and adaptability, notes another *Harvard Business Review* article author, Tim Kastelle. About time to "start reimagining management" he advises, where everyone gets a shot at becoming chief.[24]

> The employees who excel at work are not necessarily the ones who are experts or have been at the firm for a long time. They are the ones who solve problems and are very proactive in moving the organization ahead. They tend to shine and everyone wants to work with them. They are competent and have a positive attitude about work and their teammates. I think this confuses some of our tenured employees.
>
> —HR Director

It is easier for smaller companies to transition into agile businesses given the flexible environment they operate in, with reduced layers of bureaucracy. Agile firms learn and adapt quickly, swiftly responding to business forces and consumer demands. However, in waiting for approval from on high to trickle down, larger companies mired in layers of management "are trapped by their own history," thus unable to move as nimbly, notes former ManpowerGroup CEO Jeffrey Joerres. That's because "command and control behaviors" do not encourage agility. "Clearly you can't just blow your culture up. You have to figure out how to modify it so that people are able to learn and adapt. It's doable, but you have to continually break down behaviors that once worked but now get in the way," Jorres advises.[25]

Motivating a Multigenerational Workforce

Another major wrinkle (in addition to grappling with learning the digital curve, career development, plus diversity and inclusivity in the face of shifting organizational sands) is the emergence of the multigenerational workforce. As we saw in Chapter 5, five generations according to Strauss-Howe generational theory[26] working side by side is the new normal. The "17–70" workforce consists of Silent (1925–1942), Boomers (1943–1960), Generation X (1961–1981), Generation Y (aka millennials, 1982–2004), and Generation Z (2005 on) cohorts.

As it stands, only 15 percent of employees are reported to be engaged at work, a Gallup poll finds (managers, as noted previously, are engaged just 35 percent of the time). Reasons include human nature's resistance to change, businesses have not kept up training employees versus breakneck speeds of digital inventions, and the independent nature of younger employees.[27]

> I am a senior executive and have been in the workforce decades. I was in the military and worked for command control organizations. I can't understand a matrixed organization at all. It is very confusing as to who is in charge and how things get done by consensus.
>
> —Vice President, Manufacturing

Leaders need to learn and understand communication styles, expectations, work-life balances, and compensation preferences for each cohort. For example, silent and boomer generations have been groomed working in hierarchical organizations to show up on time daily, engage in face-to-face communication, and expect annual performance reviews for determining promotions and perks. However, generations X, Y, and Z generally prefer a more casual work environment and flexible conditions with time off for play (or sabbatical).[28]

Truly, the biggest reason for collision in a multigenerational workforce involves expectations. Generations Y and Z prefer flexibility regarding how, where, and when they work. Older generations prefer more stability and regularity with work patterns and departmental loyalty, rather than working in and across teams that continuously shift as noted earlier. HR is now called to "fly blind" in dealing with the 17–70 workforce.[29]

> Our organization now has five generations in the work force. Every generation is very different—each with different expectations, skills, and experiences. It is very confusing for HR leaders to figure out talent development plans that will motivate each generation. As an HR manager, I work with a range of competencies and skills. Our younger generation does not have communication skills (speaking, presenting, and writing) but excel in technology; and want all communication as text, video, or instant messages. Our more seasoned employees understand the process but are resistant to technology; they prefer face-to-face communications. It has created some confusing conflicts in our organization.
>
> —HR Manager

Many institutions are actively responding to changing social megaforces (described in Chapter 5). Flexible work options (FWOs) greenlight employees who are caregivers of the sandwich generation. For example, The University of Chicago HR guidebook explains:

- Women with young children are the fastest growing segment of the work force. Men are more involved in family and home care responsibilities. Eighty-five percent (85%) of all workers have family care responsibilities.

- Our society is aging. Twenty-five percent (25%) of all workers have elder care responsibilities.
- More focus is being placed on work and personal goals and responsibilities.

Supervisors on flexible work arrangements are to, "Apply everyday management skills, such as assuring resources are available for the tasks at hand, supporting professional development, managing performance issues, and offering clear concise communication of organizational goals and expectations and their relationship to the overall mission of the University." Ultimately, supervisors are responsible for reducing absenteeism and turnover, and to focus on increased productivity and commitment.[30]

> I am the caregiver for my aging parents. I can't move or travel for work. My manager tells me people willing to be mobile are the ones who will have opportunities for promotion. I am confused. Why can't I be promoted if I don't move around for work?
> —Individual Contributor, Marketing

Employee Retention Strategies

In addition, FWOs are great incentives to retain capable and talented human capital. The organization in turn benefits from reducing workspace costs, reducing stress among staff, and mitigating staff absenteeism.

Robert Half, the pioneer professional staffing agency founded in 1948, advises the employer must start from Day One with the intention to retain the new hire. Job satisfaction is paramount to retain employees—including at or above market wages with good benefits (paid time off, health benefits, bonuses, retirement plans). People warm to appreciation and fair treatment, and desire challenges and excitement at work. Orientation and onboarding experiences help new hires transition and learn about company culture, which also provide them ideas on how they can contribute. Mentors who are not managers help with transitions, too.

Work-life balance is essential for an employee's wellbeing, and FWOs are proving their worth. Professional development revitalizes people and productivity with tuition reimbursement, continuing education, and conferences. Promote teamwork and collaboration by clarifying team goals, roles, and openness with constructive feedback. Most of all, celebrate milestones. And remember to review these retention strategies every year to stay current, implementing best practices to retain stellar employees for the long haul, advises Robert Half.[31]

The Society for Human Resource Management (SHRM) suggests "re-recruiting" top performers and those at risk for leaving as a retention strategy. Start out with the premise people don't stay longer than 18 months. Identify and prioritize these persons and their reasons. For instance, if they're frustrated, what are their reasons, and counter offer with workable suggestions to make them enthusiastic to come to work every day. HR customizes retention success plans for each individual, then updates them every six months.[32]

Retaining talent is especially important today given how competitive talent hunting is. Not to mention how costly recruiting employees is, with companies shelling out an average of $4,129 per head in 2016, including about 42 days to fill a vacancy, SHRM reports.[33] Today's shifting organizational structures has an impact on the career paths of employees—in turn affecting the organization's productivity and profitability. This requires a continued focus on management and HR leadership and employee programs.

Notes

1. Dell Technologies, "Realizing 2030: Dell Technologies Research Explores the Next Era of Human-Machine Partnerships," *Cision PR Newswire*, July 12, 2017, https://www.prnews wire.com/news-releases/realizing-2030-dell-technologies-research-explores-the-next-era-of-human-machine-partnerships-300486894.html.

2. *2017 Deloitte Global Human Trends*, https://www2.deloitte.com/us/en/pages/human-capi tal/articles/introduction-human-capital-trends.html.

3. Vikram Bhalla, Susanne Drychs, & Rainer Starck, Boston Consulting Group, "Twelve Forces that Will Radically Change How Organizations Work," March 27, 2017, https://www.bcg.com/publications/2017/people-organization-strategy-twelve-forces-radical ly-change-organizations-work.aspx.

4. Ibid.

5. Paul Petrone, "Are You Part of the 27% of Orgs Spending More on Learning in 2017?" *LinkedIn The Learning Blog*, https://learning.linkedin.com/blog/learning-thought-leader ship/27--of-companies-are-spending-more-on-learning-in-2017--heres-wh.

6. Ibid.

7. Paul Petrone, "Bosses Really Matter. Here are 8 Stats that Prove It," *LinkedIn The Learning Blog*, https://learning.linkedin.com/blog/engaging-your-workforce/bosses-really-matter--here-are-8-stats-that-prove-it-.

8. Jim Harter, "Managers with High Talent Twice as Likely to be Engaged," *Gallup News*, April 2, 2015, http://news.gallup.com/poll/182225/managers-high-talent-twice-likely-en gaged.aspx.

9. Paul Petrone, "Bosses Really Matter. Here are 8 Stats that Prove It," *LinkedIn The Learning Blog*, https://learning.linkedin.com/blog/engaging-your-workforce/bosses-really-matter--here-are-8-stats-that-prove-it-.

10. Sarah Payne, "Survey: 93 Percent of Managers Need Training on Coaching Employees," globoforce.com, May 21, 2017, http://www.globoforce.com/gfblog/2017/managers-coaching-employees/.

11. Learning LinkedIn, "2018 Workplace Learning Report: The Rise and Responsibility of Talent Development in the New Labor Market," https://learning.linkedin.com/resources/workplace-learning-report-2018.

12. Ibid.

13. Ibid.

14. Delivering Happiness website, n.d., http://deliveringhappiness.com/book/.

15. Daniel Roth, "Top Companies: Where the US Wants to Work Now 2018," LinkedIn.com, March 21, 2018, https://www.linkedin.com/pulse/linkedin-top-companies-2018-where-us-wants-work-now-daniel-roth/?trk=eml-top_companies_2018.

16. Serenity Gibbons, "Many Employees have a Mid-Career Crisis. Here's How Employers Can Help," *Harvard Business Review*, March 20, 2018, https://hbr.org/2018/03/many-employees-have-a-mid-career-crisis-heres-how-employers-can-help.

17. Chrystal Doucette, "The Advantages of a Hierarchical Organizational Structure," *Chron Small Business*, n.d., http://smallbusiness.chron.com/advantages-hierarchical-organizational-structure-17309.html.

18. Zev Gotkin, "America's Innovative Companies are Going Flat," *HuffingtonPost.com*, October 17, 2012, https://www.huffingtonpost.com/zev-gotkin/corporate-hierarchy-work_b_1962345.html.

19. Ethan Bernstein, John Bunch, Niko Canner, & Michael Lee, "Beyond the Holacracy Hype," *Harvard Business Review*, https://hbr.org/2016/07/beyond-the-holacracy-hype.

20. Ibid.

21. David Gelles, "At Zappos, Pushing Shoes and a Vision," *New York Times*, July 17, 2015, https://www.nytimes.com/2015/07/19/business/at-zappos-selling-shoes-and-a-vision.html?mtrref=undefined&gwh=252E6885FD4A06980763CB4BCAA8FCED&gwt=pay.

22. Christina DesMarais, "Your Employees Like Hierarchy (No Really)," *Inc.*, August 16, 2012, https://www.inc.com/christina-desmarais/your-employees-like-hierarchy-no-really.html.

23. Eilene Zimmerman, "Jeffery Pfeffer: Do Workplace Hierarchies Still Matter?" *Stanford Business*, March 24, 2014, https://www.gsb.stanford.edu/insights/jeffrey-pfeffer-do-workplace-hierarchies-still-matter. Jeffrey Pfeffer, "You're Still the Same: Why Theories of Power Hold Over Time and Across Contexts," *Stanford Business*, November 1, 2013, https://www.gsb.stanford.edu/faculty-research/publications/youre-still-same-why-theories-power-hold-over-time-across-contexts.

24. Tim Kastelle, "Hierarchy is Overrated," *Harvard Business Review*, November 20, 2013, https://hbr.org/2013/11/hierarchy-is-overrated.

25. Amy Bernstein, "Globalization, Robots, and the Future of Work: An interview with Jeffrey Jorres," *Harvard Business Review*, October 2016, https://hbr.org/2016/10/globalization-robots-and-the-future-of-work.

26. https://en.wikipedia.org/wiki/Strauss–Howe_generational_theory.

27. Gallup, *State of the Global Workplace*, December 19, 2017, https://800ceoread.com/products/state-of-the-global-workplace?utm_source=link_newsv9&utm_campaign=item_220313&utm_medium=copy&_ga=2.138820147.1614620057.1517589005-1357903141.1517589005.

28. Lauren Helen Leyden & Grace Margaret O'Donnell, "Top 10 Topics for Directors: Managing Five Generations of Employees," January 2, 2018, https://www.akingump. com/en/experience/practices/corporate/ag-deal-diary/top-10-topics-for-directors-in-2018-managing-five-generations-of.html?utm_source=Mondaq&utm_medium=syn dication&utm_campaign=View-Original. John Rampton, "Different Motivations for Different Generations of Workers: Boomers Gen X, Millennials, and Gen Z," October 17, 2017, https://www.inc.com/john-rampton/different-motivations-for-different-generations-of-workers-boomers-gen-x-millennials-gen-z.html.

29. Kate Fletcher, "Five Generations, Flying Blind—Today's HR Challenges Greater Than Ever," Sage People, October 19, 2016, https://www.sagepeople.com/resources/press-releases/from-17-to-70-five-generations-flying-blind/.

30. The University of Chicago, *Flexible Work Options Guide for Staff Non-Union Employees*, n.d., http://humanresources.uchicago.edu/fpg/policies/300/2103%2012%2009%20Flexi leWorkOptionsGuide-U310.pdf.

31. Robert Half, "Effective Employee Retention Strategies," April 24, 2017, https://www. roberthalf.com/blog/management-tips/effective-employee-retention-strategies.

32. Adrienne Fox, "Keep Your Top Talent: The Return of Retention," SHRM, April 1, 2014, https://www.shrm.org/hr-today/news/hr-magazine/pages/keep-your-top-talent-the-return-of-retention.aspx.

33. SHRM, "Average Cost-per-Hire for Companies is $4,129, SHRM Survey Finds," August 3, 2016, https://www.shrm.org/about-shrm/press-room/press-releases/Pages/Human-Capital-Benchmarking-Report.aspx.

· 9 ·

WHERE ARE THE JOBS?

There are many more job options available today. However, individuals need to make time to research what each hiring path offers. While it may seem overwhelming at first, knowing what's out there to map out a new or changing career path will help avoid career confusion. I meet many job seekers in the course of my speaking engagements. Here is one poignant example where pre-planning a career path would have avoided career confusion.

> I had part time jobs while in college. I graduated and joined a firm. My manager says I have to think about my career. I liked it better when I only had to show up and do a job task, not have to think. How do I think about a career when I just got out of college?
> —New Hire, Healthcare firm

The process of selecting a good-fit job that develops into a satisfying career can be daunting to many, as this new graduate example shows. To put in the slog to find a job an individual is motivated to excel in, that provides the incentive to do good work, and for both employee and employer to be happy and satisfied at the end of the day, involves a thoughtful process of considering best-fit options for job seekers. The process is like trying to decide where you want to live: a sunny area, humid, mountain, desert, snow, four-season climate; house, or apartment; in a city, suburb, or rural area. It all takes time and research to find the best fit.

Career planning is another aspect of personal development; it affects our self-enrichment, not only outer remuneration, but inner satisfaction as well. A pathway may transition into new professional areas at different times if needed, to put us onto a lifelong fulfilling career pathway. Where are the good jobs and how can we prepare to find them, and to fit in as best we can?

Employment Sectors

Public employment or the first sector refers to government jobs at federal, state, and local municipal levels. The business or second sector includes firms owned by individuals from one-person shops to mega corporations like JP Morgan Chase & Co. A privately held business can take the form of a sole proprietorship, partnership, corporation, S corporation, or a limited liability corporation (LLC), very different from larger corporations privately owned like Nike, or publicly traded like IBM. The third sector of IRS tax-exempt nonprofits of which the 501(c)(3) designation is most common are focused on doing public good works benefiting communities with social services, education, environmental stewardship, and other areas.

All three primary sectors fuel hiring platforms in every world economy. Within these three primary employment sectors, various industries intersect, such as startups, entrepreneurs, family-owned firms, franchisees, and emerging "gig" and platform economies, in addition to worldwide mega corporations like Apple and Google.

The gig and platform economies are newer trends emerging in response to changing workplace demands. Employers are getting leaner and trimmer hiring employees. Many employers prefer to hire freelancers for cost savings since gigs do not come with benefits like health insurance. Freelancers prefer gigs that afford them more freedom, are 24/7 on global time, and especially convenient thanks to the Internet.[1]

Getting to know what each sector offers is worth the time and effort spent analyzing them, for the opportunities they each present. Also, keep in mind megatrends and forces (described in Chapter 5) continuously impact all sectors, thus necessitating changing work conditions. Individuals have to keep up with the latest developments of the Fourth Industrial Revolution, while honing a creative edge in adapting to stay focused and forward moving.

Where the Jobs Are

Since its founding in 1935, Gallup Poll has consistently found people the world over just want "a good job." A god job is defined as working at least 30 hours a week for an employer who can be counted on for a regular paycheck. Good jobs are the life force of a booming economy, a growing middle class, and human development. Therefore, the top priority for government and business leaders is to create good jobs for people everywhere, notes Gallup.[2]

Here's how one individual's parents went about to creatively ignite their child's search to look for a good job and, ultimately, a lifelong career that satisfies. Like any significant move, you have to start early, to begin working in practical moves that are purposefully strategic. This particular strategy encouraged the individual to learn and absorb ideas on their own turf, to decide their own best options to pursue in college, and work towards finding a good job.

> My mom and dad both worked. They always took to me to work with them so I could see what they and other people did, where they worked. I think this is important. I asked people about their jobs, how they did their jobs, why they liked or disliked their jobs. It also helped me understand before I went to college what kinds of majors I might pursue. Research is an important part of any endeavor.
>
> —Executive, Transportation Industry

The U.S. Bureau of Labor Statistics (BLS) reported 5.8 million jobs were unfilled on the last day of 2017.[3] Yet this data is incongruous with about 6.7 million unemployed Americans in February 2018.[4] Even more pernicious, apart from loss of income, unemployment issues tear at the country's socio-economic fabric—ripping apart homeownership, marriage, and retirement. AP News reported education has become the nation's socioeconomic fault line.[5] Traditionally, high school graduates were the backbone of U.S. manufacturing industries with well-paying jobs. But those jobs dried up when corporations outsourced manufacturing overseas where labor was cheaper. With homegrown jobs lost, schools eliminated vocational and technical education programs, and losing another important cog that had trained people for the skilled trades.

However, with labor costs rising abroad, and realizing skill levels are higher back home, U.S. manufacturing jobs have returned from overseas.

"Reshoring" with higher skill sets (or upskilling) is required today to keep up with the pace of new advancing technologies. Factory hires need training to handle new processes introduced by technology-based equipment.[6]

After the Great Recession (2007–2009) ended, college degree holders have recaptured most of the "new middle" jobs that pay more. In 2015, college graduates earned 56 percent more than high school graduates. These non-college graduates faced an overall 3 percent income drop along with declining job openings. Instead of pressuring kids on to college, labor economists urge parents to encourage high schoolers to train for new middle jobs that may or may not require technical or technological skills.[7]

A 2018 report by Manpower Group headlined *Skills Revolution 2.0, Robots Need Not Apply* assures us that humans still top automation. Human ingenuity combining soft skills with digital savvy for problem solving continues to be very much in demand. "We need to help people think differently, too. In this digital world, success will not always require a college degree, but will rely heavily on the appetite for continuous skills development," notes Jonas Prising, CEO of Manpower Group.[8]

I did not go to college. I learned about water heating and HVAC systems instead. I always have a job with a reputable company and I have a full time job. I really don't have to think about a career as my day is set every day and I am very busy.

—HVAC Engineer

Responses from 20,000 employers in 42 countries for Manpower Group's 2017 survey reiterated the fact that machines will not replace humans. Rather, 86 percent say they will increase hiring to augment machines. With the right skills mix, people will complement rather than compete with technology. "Human strengths include traditional soft skills such as communication, collaboration, and creativity, as well as uniquely human traits like empathy, relationship-building, cognitive ability, curiosity and the desire to learn," the report stresses.[9] Employees will have to develop curiosity and learnability, reskilling continuously.

Digitization is accelerating growth in manufacturing and production functions, with other areas following, in all 42 countries the Manpower Group surveyed. IT-related industries will increase most, with office and administrative functions least. In financial services, real estate, and insurance, IT staff will increase five times more than for accounting.[10]

In this country, Georgetown University's Center on Education and the Workforce' report on *Recovery: Job Growth Through and Education Requirements Through 2020* projects 55 million job openings through to 2020. Twenty-four million new jobs will be created and 31 million jobs from boomers retiring. Education requirements for these jobs are:

- 35 percent of job openings with at least a bachelor's degree
- 30 percent some college or an associate degree
- 36 percent will not require schooling beyond a high school diploma

The *fastest* growing U.S. jobs are in STEM, healthcare, and community services. Soft and cognitive skills such as analytical and problem skills are important in candidates.[11]

Jobs projected by BLS with the *most growth* in 2016–2026 (based on 2016 median annual wages) are:

- Personal care aides: $21,920
- Combined food preparation and serving workers: $19,440
- Registered nurses: $68,450
- Home health aides: $22,600
- Software developers, applications: $100,080
- Janitors and cleaners (not maids, housekeepers): $24, 190
- General and operations managers: $99,310
- Laborers and freight movers: $25,980
- Medical assistants: $31,540
- Wait staff: $19,990[12]

According to *Business Insider*, America's top ten *highest-paying* jobs for 2018 based on mean annual salaries are: anesthesiologist ($269,600); surgeon ($252,910); obstetrician and gynecologist ($234,210); oral and maxillofacial surgeon ($232,870); orthodontist ($228,780); physician ($201,840), psychiatrist ($194,740), pediatrician ($168,990), dentist ($159,770), and prosthodontist ($126,050).[13]

My parents sent me to a topnotch college where I had an excellent education. My father was in public service, very good with people, and community service. They thought I would get a corporate job. Instead, I wanted to be with people. I became a firefighter. I love my job and my life, to serve people as a first responder.

—Firefighter

Where are the jobs?

Figure 9.1. Source: ©Cartoon Resource.

New Middle Jobs

What about millions of job seekers who don't want to go into student debt and are happy with jobs that earn less? Currently, 30 million U.S. jobs pay well for non-college high school graduates, reports a 2017 study by Georgetown University Center on Education and the Workforce in partnership with JP Morgan Chase Co. The annual median income for "new middle" jobs is $55,000 (at least $35,000 for those 45 and younger; at least $45,000 for those 45 and older) not requiring the B.A. degree. However, specific skillsets for new middle jobs are different from previous traditional blue-collar manufacturing jobs (like assembly-line work), in a shift dictated by digital technology in combination with applied soft skill services.

Newer middle jobs do require postsecondary education, certifications, and extra training to keep up with technological advancements—with associate degree holders benefiting the most. "Americans with only high school graduation still have the largest share of good jobs (11.6 million), but that share continues to decline. Workers with some college have 9.3 million good jobs, those with Associate's degrees have 7.6 million good jobs, and high school dropouts only have 1.7 million," the Georgetown study reported.[14]

With 20 percent aging boomers retiring, firms must constantly train to keep up with a pipeline of skilled technicians. As an example, close to Minneapolis, E. J. Ajax manufactures precision equipment. Realizing the need to be proactive, 5 percent of Ajax's payroll goes to train current employees for vital skillsets projected ahead, a strategic move to fill vacancies when employees retire, to avoid missing production and delivery deadlines. Ajax further collaborated with competitors to start Precision Sheet Metal Academy to train metal toolmakers, with graduates scoring a 98 percent hiring rate.[15]

In addition, 70 percent of men consistently grabbed more of good jobs that do not require a college degree. Even with the shift toward healthcare, women have not managed to increase their share of going after good jobs. The three largest U.S. economies with the most good job openings for non-degree holders are California, Texas, and Florida.[16]

Georgetown University Center on Education for the Workforce study has an interactive online database, GoodJobsData.org. As an aside, in examining 1976–2017 data from this database, a report on why *Women Can't Win* showed women need one more degree than men to gain equal pay. Women continue to face work discrimination, inherently set up by a prevailing culture that does not encourage them to go after the most lucrative jobs. While the gender wage gap is real, workplaces need to be redesigned to accommodate women, too, the study advices. Real-time updates and reports are on twitter.com/GeorgetownCEW.[17]

The message is loud and clear. Prevailing counterproductive attitudes on education and jobs must shift, to keep up with social and technological changes. A seismic shift must occur for people to accept the fact that they do not have to get four-year degrees (that further buries them in massive student debts) to achieve career advancement, great pay, and job stability.

> My mother told me to go to college, become a lawyer, and make lots of money. In my first year, I realized I wasn't cut out for college or law. I talked to my career adviser. We looked at what kinds of jobs I might like, as I like to work with my hands. I'm also a scuba diver. We found programs for underwater welders, and they make big bucks! I transferred. I'm much happier with my new career pursuit. Mom is happy, too.
>
> —Underwater Welder

Society should recognize the value of blue-collar jobs. Employers are able to hire qualified, trained personnel. Employees are able to tap into higher paying jobs at half the cost of college tuition and related student costs. Upon high school graduation, upskilling technical and social skills can help individuals earn annual salaries of over $100,000.

Consider a New York City police officer making up to $116,000 yearly with overtime, where a sergeant draws $105,000–$131,000 plus $50,000 overtime. Bartenders in Los Angeles make $45,000–$73,000 plus tips, pulling in $100,000 a year—although the BLS lists their income at $18,900 per year. BLS lists construction managers drawing $82,790–$144,520 annually, with 57 percent self-employed. BLS lists farmers and ranchers (those who are not farm laborers) making $70,110–$119,530 each year. Foremen, supervisors, and managers at oil rigs cracked over $101,000 in 2013.[18] True blue and other blue collar jobs are gold mines for today's gold collar jobs waiting to be mined by at least 30 million job seekers.

> My dad is a tradesman. He taught me a specialized trade skill working on fireplaces and chimneys. I think it is very valuable as I am employable with plenty of jobs always available. I like to work with my hands and be outside, so it is a good fit for me.
>
> —Chimney Sweep

BLS figures for 2018 job openings project healthcare, IT and digital, construction, and long-haul drivers as top employment areas. The heavy demand for these workers is due to: (a) aging and retiring boomers, (b) lack of new graduates and skilled trade personnel in these areas, and (c) industry growth.[19]

The changing demographic of aging boomers is now hitting a critical need for more home care. Healthcare practitioners are in demand, from highly paid nurse practitioners who can top over $100,000 annually, physical therapists (31 percent and 34 percent, respectively), and lower-paying personal care and home care aides. As well, financial planners for boomers approaching retirement age to put their expenses in order.[20]

> When I started having children in my 30s, I left the workforce with no plans to return. My husband however got very ill and could no longer work. I had to return to work in my 60s after not working over 30 years. I reviewed my past work roles and assessed what skills and experiences would be most in demand for the highest paying job I could position my assets with, and came up with project management. I revised my resume and focused only on all relevant experiences. It was tough as I have lots of skills and experiences; but you need to focus on just what you're pursuing. Besides, you can talk about the rest at interviews. I next contacted some of my past managers to see if they knew of openings. One past manager, a university director, remembered me in a positive way and gave me a strong reference. Thanks to her, I was hired for a part-time contract job in project management—then full-time within the year.
> —Information Technology Project Manager, Top Tier University

The uptick for construction and long-haul drivers signals a growing U.S. economy recovering from the Great Recession of 2007–2009, when many were laid off with the economy tanking. CareerCast.com reports contractors face a 60 percent vacancy for skilled laborers, while the trucking industry needs over 175,000 drivers by 2026.[21]

Pulling figures from a combination of BLS and job databases, the Society for Human Resource Management (SHRM) projects top ten positions to fill in 2018 are:

1) Application software developer
2) Construction laborer
3) Financial advisor
4) Home health aide
5) Information security analyst
6) Medical services manager
7) Nurse practitioner

8) Personal care aide
9) Physical therapist
10) Truck driver[22]

The new talent landscape is encouraging for jobseekers willing to combine learning new skills (or learnability), soft skills, and are confident working with digital technology. The SHRM reports 68 percent of U.S. HR professionals found it hard to recruit talent in 2016. Eighty-four percent found it even harder to locate candidates with soft skills. More than two-thirds of recruiters (70 percent) now actively use social media platforms to approach prospects—and a great online strategy for jobseekers to market their online presence.[23] (More details are in the final chapter.)

In researching job data projections, *Fast Company* reports the five jobs in America that will be *hardest* to fill in 2025 are: skilled trades (welders, machinists, electricians), healthcare, manufacturing, sales, and math-related professions (IT, data analytics, statisticians).[24] Be on the lookout for skills gaps projections like this and begin planning accordingly. HR managers and CEOs are on a forward-looking trajectory recruiting for potential gaps to fill.

World Economic Forum's 2015 survey of over 350 employers in nine industries from the world's top economies projects that by 2020, the fastest growing industries are: business and financial operations; management; computer and math-related; architecture and engineering; sales; and education and training. Professions expected to decline most are: office administration; manufacturing and production; construction and extraction; the arts, design, entertainment, sports, and media; legal; and installation and maintenance.[25]

Career Opportunities

Figure 9.2. Source: ©Cartoon Resource.

Job Boards

How to begin the job search process? Online research is a good place to start, along with tapping high school career placement services and college career centers. There are literally thousands of advertised jobs posted on online job boards and staffing databases from around the world. These databases are readily accessible 24/7, with new job posts added and others periodically updated in real time.

Online searches are convenient tools for job hunters working from the convenience of home. For example, keywords like "top/best job websites" pull up Robert Half's top ten recommendations. (Robert Half pioneered professional staffing agency services in 1948.) This global firm's "10 Best Job Search Websites" in 2017[26] after listing Robert Half first, are:

- CareerBuilder, a huge job board with filters for criteria; https://www.careerbuilder.com
- Indeed, also a huge job aggregator for local and global posts; https://www.indeed.com/
- Job.com uses blockchain technology for matchups; http://www.job.com/
- TheLadders for C-suite searches starting at $100K; https://www.theladders.com/
- LinkedIn, sold to Microsoft in 2016 for $26.2 billion; https://www.linkedin.com/
- Glassdoor has employee company reviews; https://www.glassdoor.com/index.htm
- Monster started in 1999 for local and global job listings; https://www.monster.com/
- SimplyHired has a salary estimator; https://www.simplyhired.com/
- Us.jobs for state government jobs; https://us.jobs/index.asp

Job.com is the only offshore staffing database in Robert Half's top ten. Based in Singapore, it reports the overall global recruitment industry spends in excess of $638 billion annually, with the United States spending $150 billion to recruit the best candidates each year. Recruitment agencies earn huge fees, on average 20 percent of the successful candidate's salary.[27]

Truly, the Internet has become the most amazing tool for job seekers. Job boards also offer related services such as tips for building resumes, salary estimators, and interviews. Salary.com has tips on negotiating a paycheck to reflect your worth, a benefits calculator, and comparisons for cost-of-living expenses. https://www.salary.com/category/salary/

My parents both work for high tech firms. They work 24/7 and I never see them. I don't want to pursue technology or corporate jobs as a career, as I think you don't have a life or care about people. I would rather scrub toilets in Africa than succumb to the regimes of the corporate world.

—Recent Graduate, Fundraiser, Nonprofit Firm

Hitting Your Stride

Think about what you'd like to do, that you do well—and well enough to make money at it. This puts the responsibility on individuals to research, experience, and explore options to understand as much as possible about firms and industries before applying. Maximize and use the above resources as much as you can. Review them all, including others not on this list. Set up an account with at least 2–3 online job boards, and keep checking in.

If you can't think about what you want to do just yet, start eliminating jobs and industries that don't appeal to you. This will help narrow your exploration. Talk to people employed in industries and firms that interest you. Ask them questions. Make detailed notes on their answers you can further analyze and refer to periodically. Network and stay in touch, as personal contacts offer

"Do you see job openings out there?"

Figure 9.3. Source: ©Cartoon Resource.

invaluable references to their employers who are more likely to hire based on their employee's recommendations.

Informational Interviews

Set up informational interviews with people who are in jobs or industries you are interested in. An informational interview is a short, twenty-minute exploratory Q&A session in person, on the phone, or online. Start your process with these tips:

- Reflect and prepare 5–10 key questions that will help you understand the job, the industry, and the corporate or company culture.
- Preparing in advance includes reading up on the firm and the person you are talking to. Find out what the person thinks their firm is looking for in candidates.
- Send them the questions in advance, so they can have answers ready for you when you talk. Be on the alert for follow-up questions you can ask, during your conversation.

My parents wanted me to go to a topnotch school to become a doctor. So, I did. But by sophomore year I knew I was not going to be a doctor. From past summer jobs, I knew I was more interested in advertising. I had to break it to them I would not be a doctor, and switched my major midstream. I'm now a successful executive in an advertising agency. I think it is very important to understand what your unique calling is. Then try to explore it as a summer job or internship. Focus on what works for you. Otherwise, you will be very unhappy.

—Vice President, Advertising Agency

Confused?

How do you decide on a career direction when you don't know what's out there, with so much information (sometimes offering contradictory projections), and nothing is consistent but increasingly disruptive? What can you do today to plan your career steps?

1. *Locality.* If you plan to stay in your local area, focus on industries there. Try Orlando for tourism, Silicon Valley for technology; Houston for oil and gas; Detroit for automotive and related industries. This does

not mean you can't pursue other industries; this is but one practical approach to acquire an education for skills required.

2. *Firm proximity.* If you prefer a 10-minute commute, research local firms. What kinds of job will they be looking at? What industries are they in? Focus on internships and apprenticeships with these firms to pave the way.

3. *Functional area.* For instance, if you want to pursue HR, locate firms that are hiring, and how they differ firm to firm.

4. *Industry.* Healthcare, retail, law, freelance gigs, graphic design, etc.?

5. *Mobility.* Are you willing to relocate? Can you move? Many people think they can move, but in reality are tied to family, eldercare, or working spouse obligations that would make it very unrealistic to relocate.

6. *High growth opportunities.* Look at emerging technologies, and build expertise.

7. *Personal preferences.* Prefer a 9–5 job; traveling locally, regionally, or internationally?

8. *Core abilities, skills, and interests.* What are you good at? Why do you like to do what you like, and do well enough to get paid for?

9. *Education requirements.* Are you willing to take degrees and advanced degrees? Prefer to work with your hands, to learn a skilled trade instead?

10. *Evaluate careers by family career paths.* Are they lawyers, doctors, teachers? What insights can they offer you? Carrying on the family business?

11. *Determined to be an entrepreneur,* to start out on your own?

12. *Follow your hobbies.* Like to golf, cook, or care for animals? These interests might clue you in to careers you want to explore.

How to get started:

- Self-assessment; there are lots of free online exercises to help you discover what you'd like to do
- Research areas you're interested in; take notes
- Talk to people in various occupations for how-to tips; take notes
- Try out various gigs: job shadow, work part-time initially, to get a feel
- Make a plan with backups; be flexible and expect to change to Plan B if Plan A is not working out

Future-Proof Your Career Path

Admittedly, "The problem with the changing world of work is not so much the loss of opportunities as the period of transition," notes a World Economic Forum article. Transitions are complicated and can be painful to many—especially those who resist change and become overwhelmed. According to futurist Alvin Toffler, author of *Future Shock* (Random House, 1970; Bantam, 1984), individuals who are flexible *unlearning* the old and welcoming opportunities to *relearn* new ways of working will thrive.[28]

Two solutions are useful to cultivate: (a) to keep on learning and acquiring new skills, and (b) keep doing things that people need. Most of all, individuals who do well in transitioning are curious, open to new ideas, and ready to explore and experiment new options.[29] Regardless of failure (after all, failures are pillars to success), keep on striving to learn new skills to stay engaged and employable in this Fourth Industrial Revolution.

Notes

1. Vikram Bhalla, Susanne Drychs, & Rainer Starck, Boston Consulting Group, "Twelve Forces that Will Radically Change How Organizations Work," March 27, 2017, https://www.bcg.com/publications/2017/people-organization-strategy-twelve-forces-radically-change-organizations-work.aspx.

2. "Real Unemployment—Depart of Labor (U-6)," n.d., http://news.gallup.com/poll/189068/bls-unemployment-seasonally-adjusted.aspx.aspx.

3. U.S. Bureau of Labor Statistics, "Job Openings and Labor Turnover Summary," February 6, 2018, https://www.bls.gov/news.release/jolts.nr0.htm.

4. U.S. Bureau of Labor Statistics, "Employment Situation Summary," March 9, 2018, https://www.bls.gov/news.release/empsit.nr0.htm.

5. Christopher S. Rugaber, "Pay Gap between College Grads and Everyone Else at a Record," APNews.com, January 12, 2017, https://apnews.com/8ed3d9b045644d6ba48a6f9dfe0d142f/Pay-gap-between-college-grads-and-everyone-else-at-a-record.

6. MaryJo Webster, "Where the Jobs Are: The New Blue Collar," *USA Today*, September 30, 2014, https://www.usatoday.com/story/news/nation/2014/09/30/job-economy-middle-skill-growth-wage-blue-collar/14797413/.

7. Ibid.

8. Jonas, Prising, "Skills Revolution 2.0: Robots Need Not Apply," ManpowerGroup, 2018, http://www.manpowergroup.co.uk/wp-content/uploads/2018/01/MG_WEF_Skills Revolution_2.0_paper_lo.pdf.

9. Ibid.

10. Ibid.

11. Anthony P. Carnevale, Nicole Smith, & Jeff Strohl, "Recovery: Job Growth and Education Requirements Through 2020," Georgetown University Center for Education and the Workforce, June 23, 2013, https://cew.georgetown.edu/cew-reports/recovery-job-growth-and-education-requirements-through-2020/.

12. https://www.bls.gov/emp/ep_table_104.htm.

13. Rachel Gillet, "The 25 Best High-paying Jobs in America for 2018," *BusinessInsider.com*, January 10, 2018, http://www.businessinsider.com/best-highest-paying-jobs-in-america-for-2018-2018-1?r=UK&IR=T.

14. JPMorgan Chase & Co., "30 Million Workers without a Bachelor's Degree have Good Jobs Says Georgetown University Research," July 26, 2017, https://www.jpmorganchase.com/corporate/news/pr/30m-workers-without-bachelors-have-good-jobs-says-georgetown-university-research.htm.

15. Ibid.

16. Ibid.

17. Katie Kindelan, "Women Need One Degree more than Men to Earn Equal Pay, Report Finds," ABC News, March 1, 2018, http://abcnews.go.com/GMA/Living/women-degree-men-earn-equal-pay-report-finds/story?id=53420126. https://twitter.com/GeorgetownCEW.

18. Quentin Fottrell, "5 Entry-level Jobs that Pay More than $100,000 a Year," November 8, 2017, https://www.marketwatch.com/story/5-entry-level-jobs-that-pay-more-than-100000-2017-11-02#false.

19. CareerCast.com, "The Toughest Jobs to Fill in 2018," n.d., www.careercast.com/jobs-rated/toughest-jobs-to-fill-2018.

20. Ibid.

21. Ibid.

22. Roy Maurer, "These are the Hardest Jobs to Fill Right Now," SHRM, February 28, 2018, https://www.shrm.org/resourcesandtools/hr-topics/talent-acquisition/pages/hardest-jobs-to-fill-2018.aspx.

23. "The New Talent Landscape: Recruiting Difficulty and Skills Shortages," SHRM, June 21, 2016, https://www.shrm.org/hr-today/trends-and-forecasting/research-and-surveys/pages/talent-landscape.aspx.

24. Gwen Moran, "5 Jobs that will be the Hardest to Fill in 2025," *Fast Company*, July 18, 2016, https://www.shrm.org/hr-today/trends-and-forecasting/research-and-surveys/pages/talent-landscape.aspx.

25. Cadie Thompson, "8 Jobs Every Company Will be Hiring For by 2020," World Economic Forum, January 22, 2016, https://www.weforum.org/agenda/2016/01/8-jobs-every-company-will-be-hiring-for-by-2020/.

26. Robert Half, "10 Best Job Search Websites," August 11, 2017, https://www.roberthalf.com/blog/job-market/10-best-job-search-websites.

27. Job.com.

28. Laurent Haug, "How Do You Get a Job that Doesn't Exist Yet?" World Economic Forum, August 31, 2016, https://www.weforum.org/agenda/2016/08/how-to-prepare-for-work-jobs-of-future/.

29. Ibid.

· 1 0 ·

CAREER PLANNING FOR INDIVIDUALS

Undoubtedly, career planning is a vital step forward for every individual's career advancement and ongoing life enhancement. We are living longer and working longer. Many of us will be working for sixty or more years during our lifetimes. This new career landscape needs planning and foresight for life's journey. It begins with identifying a person's interests during childhood. The next steps explore options in high school with part-time work during school breaks. Then, even more concerted efforts in college to pursue and land that first professional vocation upon graduation. This chapter discusses how to future-proof your career before, during, and after joining an organization as an employee, or self-employed in starting your own business.

I'm a recruiter. I tell candidates the key is to focus only on jobs they are qualified. The trap candidates fall into is, applying for every job that sounds great. But look at it from the hiring manager's point of view, who only wants someone with the experience and skills they advertise for. That means you need to carefully read the job requirements and ask if you really have what it takes. If you don't, do not apply. Reason? There could be hundreds of highly qualified candidates pursuing the same job, who quickly rise to the top in matchups. While your resume falls into a black hole.

—Contract Recruiter

Starting Young for Career Preparation

Growing up, what did you want to be? Did your parents or caregivers encourage you wholeheartedly to pursue your dreams? The *2017 Imagination Report* surveyed over 1,000 American kids under twelve. While parents are the third most important influence on their kids' dreams, the primary influence comes from the media—from watching TV, YouTube, and movies. The second influence is "personal passion" inspired by these entertainment sources. After parents, books and school contribute to a child's career dreams.

This study sees more girls taking a shine to STEM careers at 56.6 percent, with boys tilting toward civil service jobs such as firefighters (87 percent) and police officers (49 percent). Eighty percent of girls want to become doctors; 45 percent of girls select scientist, compared to 55 percent of boys. Parents find encouragement is essential for their kids' emotional, academic, and financial successes.[1]

Parents are 92 percent confident their kids have the aptitude to achieve their dreams; two-thirds (64 percent) are financially capable of supporting their kids' dreams and one-third (36 percent) unable to do so. Overall, parents see challenges in girls arising from self-doubt, and boys their inability to focus. Parents offer emotional support, saying it is important to discuss their kids' challenges to help them handle disappointments—and to keep moving forward.[2]

> Our son is homeschooled. In addition to the curriculum, I take him on educational excursions to museums, technology or space programs, libraries, and special events. I host an international student every year so my son has male role models to look up to. He's active in sports. I have lots of at-home get-togethers for kids in the neighborhood, such as parties for making gingerbread houses, pizza, decorating Easter eggs, and video production. The get-togethers expand his network and exposure to activities, so we can see where he excels.
>
> —Small Business Owner, Mother

In a global study of over 20,000 children from Australia, Belarus, Indonesia, Russia, Switzerland, Uganda, and Zambia, among others, the World Economic Forum reports:

- Gender stereotyping starts young and is a global issue evident in every country
- Career aspirations are set at seven and change relatively little between then and 18

- Significant mismatches exist between children's career aspirations and labor demands
- Less than 1 percent meet role models from the world of work visiting their schools[3]

The report posits the importance of professionals as role models to volunteer time and expertise to visit schools and inspire youth, so schoolchildren can see and understand the array of vocations available. Face-to-face also closes gender equality gaps, as in "you can only believe what you see." Especially important for children from disadvantaged backgrounds are opportunities to learn from, and inspired by, successful role models. To send a compelling message that the vast universe of occupations is available to everyone—to gear up youth to participate in a skilled modern workforce benefiting local communities and their countries.[4]

The National Alliance for Partnership in Equity advocates introducing children to diverse cross-sections of the workforce, an invaluable exercise to know they can excel in nontraditional careers. Overcoming stereotypical notions of gender, ethnicity, socioeconomic stratification, age, locality, and other factors can set the stage for women and minorities to overcome obstacles to achieve their dream careers. In the process, African American data scientists and women software engineers would materialize into very palpable careers for youth.[5]

While my husband attended a conference in Orlando, I went to Disney World. I asked some teens in Disney attire what their roles were, as they seemed too young to be employees. They said, "Interns." I got all the information from them and called my daughter, an art history major. "You're going to be a Disney intern so we have you working," I told her. She went. She still works there and loving the magic, happily making a career of Disney World.

—Proud Mother

High School and Career Development

While dreaming about a career at a young age is a good place to start, it is never too early to start thinking about and mapping out a career development plan while still in high school. Competition is even fiercer to land jobs that pay well, with accelerating digital innovations placing a premium on soft skills, to nurture creativity and problem solving with an empathic understanding of changing consumer needs, and how to create user-friendly products.

School career counselors advise high schoolers to get a leg up on college admissions with paid or unpaid work. For example, volunteering, internships, apprenticeships, and starting a business such as lawn mowing and selling items on eBay all show a student's initiative and maturity to earn his or her way through life and school with serious work. These experiences provide stepping-stones to build up credible resumes, strengthened with references from supervisors. Writing their own resume is a useful exercise to reflect and brand their expertise; in addition, developing the ability to write well and market themselves as professionals.[6]

> I'm a big golfer, so is my son. While in high school, he started a non-profit organization. He would go door-to-door collecting old golf clubs to donate to underserved youths in our area who wanted to learn golf. I think he is destined to be a business owner, like his dad.
> —Business Owner, Accounting

USA Test Prep advises high schoolers to begin developing career plans to include at least these five elements:

1. Decide on a career path that appeals, to get started working toward future goals
2. Research and understand what expectations are involved in that particular field
3. Create practical pathways to realize career goals; enroll in free online courses and other learning opportunities to hone skills, to become valuable potential hires to employers
4. Start promoting education and personal assets with a polished resume to include testimonials from supervisors; start looking for jobs before graduating on a regularly scheduled basis; and discuss progress reports with parents, teachers, or school career counselors
5. Be practical and patient in not being discouraged about being hired immediately; stay on course, and continue to hone skills in various areas to show your worth to employers.[7]

Students must start taking responsibility for career development early. The *New York Times'* columnist and author Thomas Friedman reported the College Board analyzed results of 250,000 graduating high schoolers in 2017 who took both the new PSAT and new SAT. Students who went on to take free personalized improvement practices through Khan Academy saw dramatic increases in their SAT scores. After 20 hours of practice, they improved by an average of 115 points—doubling the score for those who did not practice self-improvement.[8] The onus in getting ahead is definitely upon the individual, along with the determination for lifelong learning.

Millennial Branding and Internships.com found high schoolers in 2014 were more career-focused compared to college students. Internships and volunteering are invaluable for college admission credentials, including finding future jobs. High schoolers seek internships to get new skills (92 percent), work experience (81 percent), and mentoring/networking (72 percent). In addition, 70 percent of companies say high schoolers completing internship programs are more likely to land college internships with them, with 45 percent high school internships morphing into full-time work at their companies.[9]

At Lincoln Northeast High School in Nebraska, *U.S News & Reports* finds all four years of high school well spent on career development. It starts with mapping out college prep at eighth grade to see them through to high school graduation, working toward college graduation. As high school freshmen, students are pushed to start taking harder courses (instead of waiting until junior or senior years), research scholarships, and prepping the scholarship resume. They set foot on college campuses in sophomore year, attend college fairs, and further flesh out resumes with extracurricular, volunteer, and leadership activities. Juniors seek internships, job shadows, and summer jobs in alignment with their career goals and interests. Seniors focus on improving test scores for college; advanced placement testing is icing on the cake in getting ahead as a well-prepared college student headed for graduation and the world beyond.[10]

Teenagers need to learn to start taking responsibility for their own career development. Articulating career plans can help them communicate personal likes and dislikes, to be clear about decisions, become flexible and adaptable in adjusting to changes midstream, and to feel good in planning their own futures. Certainly, anyone who actively participates in acting upon their own career plans is more likely to stay the course—instead of a parent writing up their career plans for them.

I'm in my 20s and don't come from a wealthy family. When I applied to firms, I made sure they had tuition reimbursement programs so I could attend college. I know higher education separates me from the pack. Its working out well. I completed a B.A. and working on my MBA.

—Marketing Manager

"Sigh, they start on a career path so young these days."

Figure 10.1. Source: ©Cartoon Resource.

Career Prepping During College

Having started the momentum to pursue career development options and potential job opportunities at high school, college students should continue and not let up on their career pathways. Graduates must have practical professional skills to succeed. IBM reported 70 percent of corporate college recruiters found graduates-to-be lacking in:

- Critical analysis and problem solving
- Collaboration and team work
- Ability to communicate within the business context
- Adaptability, flexibility, and agility[11]

Suggestions to remedy these soft skill gaps include experience-based learning with internships, apprenticeships, and mentoring. Students should take the initiative to understand what businesses require in their employees. Find out how businesses are successful or not, then think about areas to complement or supplement need-based opportunities. Participate in job shadowing, and take relevant college classes to prepare for entry-level jobs.

> My son is in his first year of college. I called to find out if they would help him with a summer internship. It was not clear they would, so I went ahead and set up interviews for spring break.
> —Caring Mother

Additionally, graduates who understand the need for broader mindsets and worldviews when applying their skills are highly desired. For instance, IT graduates who demonstrate their knowledge across a variety of platforms—e.g., cybersecurity, e-commerce, integration, and data analytics—while at the same time staying abreast of innovations spinning out at dizzying speeds, and even working on foreign shores and learning new languages to expand their competencies, will advance quickly.[12]

> My husband and I take our daughter everywhere we go. We want her to interact with adults and learn how to socialize gracefully. She spends summers in Europe with my family or India with his, so she'll have an international perspective and learn foreign languages.
> —Real Estate Developer

A *Forbes* contributor advises students to work with college career centers upon enrolling to continue planning their career paths. Start early. Ask if the school has business partnerships to apply. Research and utilize online learning tools to get familiar with industry terms; many are free, and helpful to indicate industry experience and mastery on resumes. A problem with college graduates is they don't know what they're good at; taking online assessment tests can help identify and narrow choices for optimal career satisfaction. Network with professors and peers to possibly land jobs, either part-time while still in college, or upon graduation.[13]

> I worked unloading soda trucks for one summer job. Man, was it hard work! I decided then to do very well in college and graduate school to hold higher-paying desk jobs.
> —Executive, Management Consulting firm

With social media platforms paramount as effective tools for networking today, clean up and regularly update your profile. Create a personal website.

Start blogging to show your learning experiences and expertise gained while training at an apprenticeship or job shadow; contribute and comment on LinkedIn, the largest professional networking platform.

A traditional resume includes: (a) education, (b) related work experiences, (c) skills and competencies, and (d) hobbies/extracurricular activities. While college students may not have had a slew of jobs, they can highlight "transferable skills" suitable for professional environments. Again, sterling references are invaluable, including a reference letter from a professor; and run it by the school's writing center for a truly professional resume presentation.[14]

I worked in retail during high school summer breaks. It was useful. I realized I did not like retail hours. I also found I don't like working with people as they can be uncourteous and abrupt.

—Individual Contributor, Nonprofit

I worked in retail for my summer jobs and loved it. I liked working with customers, and viewed my associates as close family.

—Retail Manager

Continuously exploring occupational experiences helps motivated graduates move ahead with their own unique personalized career plans. Career planning is definitely a huge slice of a person's professional development to achieve lifelong success, for personal and job satisfaction. Apple Computer cofounder Steve Jobs urged, "Your work is going to fill a large part of your life, and the only way to be truly satisfied is to do what you believe is great work. And the only way to do great work is to love what you do. If you haven't found it yet, keep looking. Don't settle. As with all matters of the heart, you'll know when you find it. And, like any great relationship, it just gets better and better as the years roll on. So keep looking until you find it. Don't settle."[15]

The world's richest man and Amazon founder Jeff Bezos pushes on phenomenally because, "In the end, we are our choices. Build yourself a great story."

Professionally Yours

Truly, "Learning never exhausts the mind," advised Leonardo da Vinci who painted the *Mona Lisa* and *The Last Supper*. Even after college graduation, continue learning to build your own great story. In a crowded field with every

"I've been trying to get my resume around."

Figure 10.2. Source: ©Cartoon Resource.

job vacancy attracting about 250 resumes, it pays to spend time and creativity to craft an outstanding job resume. Be selective in your application process because it is pointless to apply to many jobs using one generic resume. Start with a stellar resume tailor-made for the job you're applying to—every time. Quickly and pointedly highlight your strengths and experiences to dove-tail with advertised job requirements. Practice makes perfect; never give up researching and applying.[16]

Along with the resume, spend time customizing, going over and over your cover letter—a one-page, single-spaced pitch. Keep writing, rewriting, editing, and curating nuggets to spin your amazing qualifications and experiences into a perfect fit to WOW HR and potential managers. Shine your brand irresistibly. "Simplicity is the ultimate sophistication," affirms da Vinci.

> When I make a job move, I'm very focused. When I send out three resumes, usually two employers respond. I research firms first, focusing only on jobs I'm highly qualified for. If I don't see one, I don't apply. In one month, I may send 2–4 resumes tailored specifically to jobs as advertised, with customized cover letters. My recommendation is, spend 80 percent of your time researching jobs, and 20 percent customizing your resume and cover letter, to make them highly targeted to requirements as advertised.
>
> —Director, Information Technology

Research shows referred job applicants are more likely hired, and enjoy longer tenure. Powerful testimonials from supervisors to show-and-tell are effective, too.[17] Another study found 30–50 percent of hiring comes from personal referrals, with referred candidates four times more likely to succeed than those not referred. According to Lou Adler, founder of his eponymous staffing agency, his firm's 2016 survey of over 3,000 respondents found a whopping 85 percent of critical jobs filled through networking. The implications are clear—spend as much time applying as with networking on your job search.[18]

Why is networking important to land jobs? Birds of a feather flock together. Spend time meeting people and talking up your career goals. Prep a 30-second elevator speech about your background; clearly explain how it benefits employers. Rehearse your delivery in front of a mirror. Practice over and over again to smooth out voice inflections and nervous facial twitches for a flawless presentation, to achieve a pleasant and natural pitch. Practice smiling warmly and genuinely. People gravitate toward people whom they feel are trustworthy, like, and can depend on to get the job done, and well. When a resume contains references from other people they know, this raises the candidate's profile even higher. It might be worthwhile to practice reconnecting with acquaintances from the past first, to gauge your delivery, before taking the plunge with new people.[19]

> I've always enjoyed playing the piano, and taught during summer breaks while still in high school. Today, I continue teaching the piano. Students either come to me, or I go to them. I don't need to advertise. My students recommend me to their friends. It's very rewarding to run my business doing something I have always enjoyed.
>
> —Music Teacher, Business Owner

Apart from dedicating time and positive energy to the application process and being involved in personal networking, a third important strategy for job seekers is to amplify your online presence in purposeful ways. In 2018 and onward, with data analytics becoming even more entrenched as a hiring tool used by HR, your online presence is an asset. Hays Group, a global specialist recruitment agency, predicts if you're optimizing your online presence, recruiters will approach you instead. Updating profiles using keywords is still essential. However, participating in social media with original posts and commenting with innovative ideas and insights shows online networking marketing savviness.[20]

LinkedIn (linkedin.com) has over 500 million global members, connecting professionals and employers who post their profiles onsite. A "gated-access community," members invite others to join as "connections." The *New York Times* notes even U.S. high schoolers are creating LinkedIn profiles and participating with comments to support their college applications.[21]

Digital resumes are another current wave of the future increasingly attracting job applicants. For instance, Sketchfab (sketchfab.com) offers 3D and robotics presentations to display creative virtual reality projects that jobseekers can showcase for prospective employers to view. Augmented virtual reality pieces will also animate resumes.[22]

Managing Your Career Development

Clearly, career development is a dynamic process that engages a person's personal and professional development with the goal of enhancing lifelong career advancement, with ongoing learning taking center stage, and your dedicated pursuit as a jobseeker shining a light on your talents on how you truly benefit prospective employers. For individuals, job hopping is the recipe for reaping richer payouts holding out for salary increases on the move. Staying put at one company locks you into small annual pay raises. Korn Ferry reports 2018 will be the seventh straight year of 3 percent median base salary raises across most U.S. industries.[23]

> When I got out of the military, I didn't know what to do. I liked cooking but unsure if it could become a career. I went to a five-star hotel and offered to work without pay one summer, in exchange for training in the kitchen. I loved it. The hotel offered me a full-time job.—Chef

Figure 10.3. Source: ©Cartoon Resource.

Today's game-changing hiring environment encourages companies to value talent and experience; hence, most are eager to raise the bar with higher starting salaries for new hires. For instance, *Forbes* calculated that staying with the same company over two years will slice off more than half your lifetime earnings (in itself a conservative estimate). Thus, starting at $55,000 with the 3 percent annual raise would only land $63,760 after five years.[24] Whereas, job hoppers unafraid to take risks and can stomach job seeking as a sideline, plus a steady investment risk in enhancing self-worth, would keep on earning more than peers locked into staying on at one firm.

> After graduating from college with a business degree, I applied online to a bunch of jobs. I took the first one that accepted me, as I needed to work, in a large healthcare private practice. I have to learn a lot every day. I will give it my best shot, but do not think this is the right field, and will keep looking for a good fit job.
>
> —Individual Contributor, Healthcare firm

Playing it like a career development pro can take on other forms, too. Run your career like a business. For example, becoming an "intrapreneur" earns an employee extra perks with the ability to dream up profitable innovations for the company. An intrapreneur is motivated like an entrepreneur to take risks in innovating for rewards. Companies liken them to secret weapons.[25]

It pays to act like a startup, as well. Regularly assess and diversify your skills to gain a unique competitive advantage. Keep on learning something fresh and new daily. Sharpen your chops from being driven by a sense of urgency to stay ahead, like any startup primed to succeed. In a world that's constantly changing, and at breakneck speed, taking risks intelligently is necessary. Being curious and confident puts you ahead in being at the right place, at the right time.[26] Stay alert, and be prepared to seize moments of serendipity to advance your career.

Become indispensable to your boss. Be the go-to person, or his/her right hand. Do make your boss look great (without brownnosing). Evaluate your skills in alignment with the firm's goals for the year, and show your worth in signing up for those projects.[27]

Lateral moves help job hoppers make great strides. These are wonderful opportunities to position transferable skills to another company or industry (in addition to increasing wages, as discussed earlier). Or getting out of toxic situations, moving out before being laid off, or to acquire new skills in a different or related industry.[28]

Modern apprenticeships are no longer the monopoly of trade guilds. The *Chicago Tribune* reports a new trend to earn-and-learn in financial services, and a smart way to avoid student debt while providing in-house specialty skilling needs for firms' own needs. Aon, the global insurance and risk management giant, offers two-year programs for positions that had previously hired only college graduates. Aon apprentices work four days onsite (tech help desk, HR, or compliance); take classes one day a week at a community college with free tuition; and draw $38,500 annually. Other banking institutions with similar apprenticeships include JP Morgan Chase and Zurich USA.[29]

Everyone in my family—mother, father, aunts, uncles—are doctors. It was inevitable for me, too. I pursued plastic surgery. Growing up with family role models doing what they like, and they involve you, you're naturally groomed to be in the same field. An apple doesn't fall far from the tree.

—Plastic Surgeon

Myriad options abound for occupational opportunities. Job seekers only have to research industries and companies they like to pursue—then tailor job applications to align with firms' current focus. Or research voids and holes to fill with scarce skills they ably bring to the table. In all likelihood, even with robots seemingly displacing humans, new jobs are constantly created to meet shifting supply chain and workforce needs. So that a changing work landscape actually reflects scarce skills, not scarce jobs, writes James Bessen in his book, *Learning by Doing: The Real Connection Between Innovation, Wages, and Wealth* (Yale University Press, 2015).

> I'm a K–12 teacher. My brother, sister, and mother are also K–12 teachers. I did not think about what my career would be. We all enjoy teaching different subjects and have lots in common, and love kids.
>
> —Teacher, Sixth Grade

Encore Careers, Second Acts

At age 63, Judy Nelson had an epiphany. She could no longer endure three-hour commutes each way, that she had done for the past 30 years, driving into the city to lead nonprofits. She promptly resigned her executive position. However, for an intelligent person, staying idle is hard to do. Finally, she figured out to transfer her leadership skills to become an executive coach.[30]

Nelson's story is actually quite common. The American Institute for Economic Research 2015 study on *New Careers for Older Workers* report that since Americans are living longer today, they work longer, too. Many delay retirement. However, there are two distinct categories, those eager and those fearful to make career changes. Those looking forward to late-life career changes report being happy doing so; 82 percent respondents indicate successful transitions after age 45. For those happy about late-life career changes (and in a marked reversal from high schoolers and college graduates) these seniors say they:

- do not take online classes, 77 percent
- do not receive a grant or scholarship to start a new job, 97 percent
- do not use formal networking channels such as LinkedIn and career fairs, 84 percent
- do not volunteer in hopes of becoming paid employees, 90 percent[31]

Second career acts typically transition within 18 months. Advance planning is key, advises a *New York Times* article. Prepare for trade-offs to be enriched in new ways, such as less stress on the job and a reduced paycheck that's balanced with rewarding outcomes. Look out for retraining requirements that are different for each industry. Network and find out what appeals to your tastes and skills. Learn from mentors who are a decade younger (sometimes lots more).[32]

> In my late 50s now, I got laid off in my late 40's in manufacturing. A single dad with three children, I thought to start a business, but found out how much time, money, and technology it took. I looked at traditional options that fit my background, and was hired by an oil refinery. My employer was impressed by my military background. The firm is hierarchical and my work hands on. I'm a union member which works with my life, skills, background. I enjoy the work and security.
>
> —Individual contributor, Oil and Gas Industry

Nonprofit websites such as Encore.org and ReServe Program provide creative ideas on how active seniors can contribute meaningfully to community needs. ReServe notes 10,000 Americans turn 65 every day. These seniors have accumulated a wealth of skills and problem-solving experiences urgently needed to fill critical talent pools for government and social services agencies. Services include addressing poverty, skills gaps, college readiness, professional coaching, and a host of other education voids.[33]

Universities such as Stanford, Harvard, Notre Dame, and the Universities of Texas and Minnesota are rolling out encore studies programs. Seniors looking to regain career traction in newer, unexplored areas hope these are personally more fulfilling this time round. However, funding poses challenges, as for anything new and untried, and only a strong vision prevails.[34]

At the end of the day, Americans are taking encore careers seriously. Researchers at the University of Michigan Retirement Research Center find 40 percent of respondents had started moving to new careers after turning 55. However, by age 62, 57 percent no longer actively work.[35]

> I am in my seventies and still working. I think you need to manage your career around your age. Work for age-appropriate firms. When I was young, startups made a lot of sense. As I matured, I looked for workplaces with more people my age in healthcare, education, nonprofit, and the public sector.
>
> —Consultant, Public Sector

Career Planning Smarts

- Start career planning early. Encourage children to dream about their career aspirations.
- Encourage high schools to offer career counseling and planning services.
- Encourage college students to resource and network with their schools' career centers.
- Be creative with resumes; consider digital and 3D versions if appropriate.
- To maintain a jobseeker's competitive edge, act like a driven entrepreneur to succeed.
- Job hops are lucrative in working toward higher remuneration with each new position.
- Stay positive and never ever give up trying, and submitting, amazing job applications.
- Honor Amazon founder Jeff Bezos' tip: "In the end, we are our choices. Build yourself a great story."

In my 50s now, I had spent my career in nursing, a physically taxing industry. I pursued classes, certifications, and degrees early in my career as I realized the need to shift to the education side or the business side when I got older. Today, I manage a hospital. Look at your industry and plan for the future, especially one that's physically taxing. Invest in what you need to do to get there, to stay on track, and to keep on learning for the joy of discovering new ideas.

—CEO, Hospital

Notes

1. Fatherly.com, "The 2017 Imagination Report: What Kids Want to Be When They Grow Up," December 22, 2017, https://www.fatherly.com/love-money/work-money/the-2017-imagination-report-what-kids-want-to-be-when-they-grow-up/.
2. Ibid.
3. Nick Chambers, "Thousands of Kids Were Asked to Draw Their Ideal Jobs—With Surprising Results," January 21, 2018, World Economic Forum, https://www.weforum.org/agenda/2018/01/kids-draw-their-future-jobs-careers/.
4. Ibid.
5. National Alliance for Partnerships in Equity, "Role Models and Mentors," n.d., https://www.napequity.org/resources/role-models/.
6. USA Test Prep, "How to Prepare Your High School Student for a Career," September 28, 2017, https://www.usatestprep.com/blog/2017/09/28/preparing-your-high-school-student-for-a-career/.

7. Ibid.

8. Thomas Friedman, "Owning Your Own Future," *New York Times*, May 10, 2017, https://www.nytimes.com/2017/05/10/opinion/owning-your-own-future.html?mcubz=0.

9. Dan Schawbel, "The High School Careers Study," February 3, 2014, Millennial Branding, http://millennialbranding.com/2014/high-school-careers-study/.

10. Kelsey Sheehy, "Use All 4 years of High School to Prep for College," *U.S. News & World Report*, September 9, 2013, https://www.usnews.com/education/blogs/high-school-notes/2013/09/09/use-all-4-years-of-high-school-to-prep-for-college.

11. Alexandra Levit, "4 Ways to Prepare for a Career While You're in College," *U.S. News & World Report*, November 6, 2015, https://money.usnews.com/money/blogs/outside-voices-careers/2015/11/06/4-ways-to-prepare-for-a-career-while-youre-in-college.

12. Ibid.

13. Drew Hendricks, "6 Ways College Students Can Better prepare for a Career in Business," *Forbes*, March 11, 2015, https://www.forbes.com/sites/drewhendricks/2015/03/11/6-ways-college-students-can-better-prepare-for-a-career-in-business/2/#2cdc3caa496c.

14. Allison Saunders, "How to Prepare for a Career While You're in College," *ZING! By Quicken Loans*, August 14, 2017, https://www.quickenloans.com/blog/prepare-career-youre-college.

15. http://www.businessinsider.com/steve-jobs-quotes-2014-4.

16. Alison Doyle, "15 Quick Tips to Get Hired Fast," thebalance.com, March 8, 2018, https://www.thebalance.com/tips-to-help-you-get-hired-fast-2059661.

17. Meta Brown, Elizabeth Setren, & Giorgio Topa, "Do Informal Referrals Lead to Better Matches? Evidence from a Firm's Employee Referral System," IZA Discussion Paper No. 8175. https://ssrn.com/abstract=2441471.

18. https://louadlergroup.com/new-survey-reveals-85-of-all-jobs-are-filled-via-networking/.

19. http://www.trivalleyonestop.org/network-way-next-job/.

20. http://www.hays.com/about-hays/index.htm.

21. https://en.wikipedia.org/wiki/LinkedIn.

22. Joe Durbin, "Get the Job: Virtual Reality Portfolios and Resumes Have Arrived," March 14, 2017, https://uploadvr.com/now-can-really-stand-putting-resume-vr/.

23. Korn Ferry, "Here We Go Again: 3 Percent Base Salary Increases Forecasted to Continue in2018," August 24, 2017, https://www.kornferry.com/press/here-we-go-again-3-percent-base-salary-increases-forecasted-to-continue-in-2018-according-to-korn-ferry/.

24. Rebecca Safier, "Why Job Hopping May be the Secret to a Bigger Salary," Student Loan Hero, April 5, 2017, https://studentloanhero.com/featured/job-hopping-higher-income/.

25. https://en.wikipedia.org/wiki/Intrapreneurship.

26. Martin Zwilling, "7 Ways and Why to Treat Your Career Like a Startup," *Forbes*/Entrepreneur, February 19, 2012, https://www.forbes.com/sites/martinzwilling/2012/02/19/7-ways-and-why-to-treat-your-career-like-a-startup/#30f037be55d8.

27. Gwen Moran, "How to Become Indispensable at Work This Year," *Fast Company*, January 12, 2018, https://www.fastcompany.com/40509085/how-to-become-indispensable-at-work-this-year.

28. Vicki Salemi, "When Should You Consider Making a Lateral Move?" *U.S. News & World Report*, August 15, 2017, https://money.usnews.com/money/blogs/outside-voices-careers/articles/2017-08-15/when-should-you-consider-making-a-lateral-move.

29. Alexia Elejalde-Ruiz, "Apprenticeship Programs Increasingly Put Workers on Track for Jobs in Finance," *Chicago Tribune*, April 24, 2017, http://www.chicagotribune.com/business/ct-aon-finance-apprenticeship-0425-biz-20170424-story.html.

30. Judy Nelson, "How I Found My Encore Career (and Why You Should)," NextAvenue.org, September 26, 2014, https://www.nextavenue.org/how-i-found-my-encore-career-and-why-you-should/.

31. American Institute for Economic Research, 2015, https://www.aier.org/sites/default/files/Files/Documents/Webform/AIER_OWS.pdf.

32. Marci Alboher, "A Switch at Midlife, to Make a Difference," *New York Times*, December 8, 2012, https://www.nytimes.com/2012/12/09/jobs/switching-careers-at-midlife-to-make-a-difference.html.

33. http://www.reserveinc.org/who-we-are.

34. Chris Farrell, "Coming Soon: 2 New Encore Career Programs at Colleges," *Forbes*, March 22, 2018, https://www.forbes.com/sites/nextavenue/2018/03/22/coming-soon-2-new-encore-career-programs-at-colleges/#7c527cef1bd3.

35. Sonnega, Amanda, Brooke Helppie McFall, & Robert J. Willis. (2016). "Occupational Transitions at Older Ages: What Moves are People Making?" Ann Arbor, MI. University of Michigan Retirement Research Center (MRRC) Working Paper, WP 2016-352. http://www.mrrc.isr.umich.edu/publications/papers/pdf/wp352.pdf.